STARTING UP YOUR OWN BUSINESS

101 ways to do it on £5000 or less

ROSS McBENNETT

MERCURY

First published in 1990
by the Mercury Books Division of
W.H. Allen & Co. Plc
Sekforde House, 175/9 St. John Street, London EC1V 4LL

Set in Concorde by Phoenix Photosetting
Printed and bound in Great Britain by
Butler & Tanner Ltd, Frome, Somerset

British Library Cataloguing in Publication Data
McBennett, Ross, *1959–*
Starting up your own business: 101 ways to do it on £5000 or less.
1. Great Britain. Small firms. Organisation
I. Title
658.0220941

ISBN 1–85252–075–2

CONTENTS

PREFACE

My starting-point for writing this book was that of a self-employed person who had made mistakes; I was convinced that most if not all of those mistakes could have been avoided if I had had access to better advicc in my early days of trading. Perhaps I thought I was too small a business to be of interest to the enterprise agencies; whatever the reason, I was shy of asking them for help. I did look for books to help me through those difficult days, but the books I looked at always seemed to be dealing with the very problems I did not face. Besides, they were usually written by senior bankers or accountants, who gave a strong impression of having forgotten what it was like to be in business, if they ever knew. Such people were inevitably obsessed (or so it seemed to me) with the problems of raising finance, but curiously silent on the day-to-day issues of bringing in new business or the equally important decision of what kind of business to go in for in the first place.

So there seemed to be a need for this kind of book – a book written in a down-to-earth style and aimed at the majority of the newly self-employed, rather than the few with special capital needs; a book with a positive and inspirational approach to the wealth of opportunities available, with enough clear and simple advice to allow the budding entrepreneur to handle his or her own accounts; above all, a book which cut through the huge mass of bewildering and often conflicting information available, to give readers only what they really needed to know to set up and run a business on limited capital for the vital first year. Of course, more specialized information may be needed on certain points, and where appropriate I have suggested suitable reading matter or organizations to contact. But the ground rules will remain the same whatever the business; it is more important in the first instance to digest those ground rules and base everything else upon them.

One final point. I have tried to ensure that any advice of a legal or technical nature is accurate at the time of going to press, but since laws change with bewildering rapidity, you would do well to check any specific points of this nature, either with the local Citizens' Advice Bureau or enterprise agency, or one of the organizations listed in the appendix to the book.

It should go without saying that a large number of individuals and organizations have helped with the researching of this book. If I attempt to name them all, I am sure to fail, so I hope they will accept this general thank you, and my assurance that I alone am responsible for any opinions or facts expressed. I must, however, single out my wife Jane, who has always encouraged me in my belief that I could write this book, and has supported me in far more ways than I had any right to expect. I hope that the finished product will convince her that it was not entirely a waste of time.

Ross McBennett
March 1990

PART I
Starting up your business

1

THINKING IT THROUGH

So you want to set up in business?

You are not alone. You might be an unemployed school-leaver or a housewife with new time on her hands, a redundant steel-worker or a new graduate, a manager bored with early retirement or a mid-career executive fed up with the rat-race. What you have in common is a feeling that you would rather be working for yourself, running your own business. But for that, you would not have picked up this book in the first place.

You are not alone. It is worth repeating: of all the problems facing the would-be entrepreneur, the sense of being alone, of having nobody to talk things over with, is perhaps the strongest. All too often it can seem as if you and your dreams of financial success and personal fulfilment are pitted against the world, that nobody understands your particular brilliant money-making idea because nobody has ever done anything like it before. Your family are starting to get nervous about where the next mortgage repayment is coming from, your friends have stopped asking you out for a drink because they are too embarrassed to ask you how the business is going, and suddenly self-employment does not seem the wonderful idea it did when you first thought of it in the bath six months earlier.

It does not have to be like that – there is certainly no shortage of people and organizations ready to help you when you run into problems, and since there really is nothing new under the sun, it is more than likely that somebody can be found who has been through your problem before.

So at the start of your enterprise, you need some initial guidelines: is self-employment really the right thing for you, have you thought your business idea through properly, does the thought of preparing a business plan scare you silly (it does most people)? What you need is a kind of guardian angel for the initial stages of your business, something which will point you in the direction of more specialist advice where required, but which will provide you with enough general information to set up and run your business for the first year. That is the gap which this book seeks to fill.

A word about the scope of the book. It assumes a £5000 capital limit for the types of ventures it will be discussing. That figure should not be treated too literally, but it will exclude some important business categories – most manufacturing and most established franchises, for example. There is certainly no intention of trying to discourage those with access to larger amounts of capital from going into business in those categories, and a good deal of what is said may be useful to them as well. But this book's purpose is slightly yet significantly different: to demonstrate that it is perfectly possible for the ordinary man or woman from any background whatsoever to set up and run his or her own business successfully without needing to borrow huge amounts of money, and certainly without having to risk everything.

Some of the types of business will need hardly any capital at all to set them in motion; others will need the full £5000, if not more. But do be careful if you think you have a brilliant idea which will cost absolutely nothing to set up – even if there are no office and equipment costs, it is rather unlikely that income will start to roll in from day one. It will take a while to get established; how long will depend partly on you, partly on the nature of the business. In the meantime you will be receiving no state benefits (with the possible exception of the Enterprise Allowance) and you and your family will need to live. Do not forget this basic point – more about it later on.

To repeat once again: you are not alone. More and more people want flexibility in their working lives. Men want to share more fully in the lives of their families and the upbringing of their children; women cannot see why their child-bearing function should any longer deny them access to fulfilling careers as well. The traditional government goal of full employment fits very uneasily with these aspirations and there is sure to be less emphasis on it. This could lead to benefits for those who are 'unemployed' as the divisions between those 'in work' and 'out of work' become less clear – the social stigma attached to 'unemployment' may also begin to break down.

New technology may even create new opportunities at the same time as it destroys conventional jobs. For example, giant concerns may no longer be interested in manufacturing items for which demand is limited. The urge to possess the unique or the rare does not really clash with inexorable trends towards mass production, for those very trends have indeed spawned that search for the unique, which might almost be seen in terms of a retreat into a more private world.

So in future more and more people are going to find themselves creating and developing their own work opportunities (a better term than 'job'). About the only thing economists agree on is that fewer and fewer will be working long shifts in the factories of the traditional 'smokestack' industries on which the British economy once depended: textiles, shipbuilding, cars. At the same time fewer will be holding down the nine to five office jobs in large bureaucracies, which once also seemed normal. Of course many will continue to be employees, but they will work in smaller organizations where money is spent on technical developments rather than on people, and where they will be employed for their specialist know-how rather than their physical labour. At the same time, the much-trumpeted service sector of the economy is likely to continue to grow; indeed, it may be that you are already well aware of this and are for that reason poised to establish your own niche within it. For services can indeed be set up fairly quickly, and generally require relatively little capital.

Opportunities for the self-employed are remarkably diverse. The most obviously promising areas at the moment are in the financial services industry and its related activities, in specialist retailing or consultancy, catering and tourism, new technology, cleaning services, skilled crafts and techniques. The traditional small-business areas – retail, building, farming and the professions – are much less likely to be growth areas. One feature of the huge economic changes of the last fifteen years has been a clarification of potential markets; it is now much easier to spot what might be viable, much more difficult to run a business inefficiently in a declining sector.

But the diversity is not confined to the nature of the work. Even within the small-business/self-employed sector the stereotypes are taking a battering. In October 1988 the Small Business Research Trust published a fascinating profile of this fastest-growing sector of the economy, suggesting, for example, that working for yourself may even be less stressful (and more conducive to a successful marriage) than working for other people. The report certainly highlights the dangers of generalizing about a small-business 'sector'.

Even at the most basic level, there are of course many different ways of being self-employed: you can be part-time, freelance, a sole trader or a partner with somebody else in business premises, the member of a small co-operative, or you can be a working director or shareholder in a small limited company. Whatever the kind of work you ultimately decide on, whatever the structure you will be operating through, you must start with yourself.

Your situation

The beginning of this chapter referred to a few common situations, one of which you may now be finding yourself in. Now look at these a little more closely – do you recognize yourself in one of the following categories?

The unemployed school-leaver

There is little work available near you. You have been on YTS schemes, swept up and made the tea, but have not learnt very much and there has been no sign of a job. Your parents and teachers tell you the discipline of 'clocking on' will stand you in good stead, but you would rather have more control over your own work. Maybe you could never pass exams, or maybe the ones you passed are not so useful in today's job market. You have no money, but you think you might as well have a go at working for yourself, perhaps with one or two of your mates. You have heard that because you are unemployed you will be eligible for an Enterprise Allowance of £40 per week for the first year, and figure that in view of this, you really do have nothing to lose.

The housewife

The kids are off your hands now, and you need ways to fill your extra time. You have never been much interested in voluntary work, and in any case you want to earn some money for yourself. You do not have a lot of spare cash, but you are already financially secure and it would not be the end of the world if you found yourself without a living wage. On the other hand you know that your experience of bringing up a family could be very valuable in business, you want to show what you can do, and get your husband and children to take and treat your ideas seriously.

The redundant worker

You have a few thousand pounds in redundancy money, and absolutely no chance of a conventional job in your locality. Some of your friends went to work down south, but returned disillusioned when they saw the cost of housing. You are fed up spending your time sitting around; you have plenty of ideas for spending the money, but you want to be sure of getting somewhere with one of them.

The pensioner

You retired, possibly early, perhaps against your will, and you lack the money to do the things you want to. You would like to earn a bit more from your own endeavours; you are uncertain as to whether you want to work full-time or for just a few hours every week.

The frustrated executive

Maybe the thrill of your first BMW is starting to pall, and you are fed up with office politics. Your loyalty is not reciprocated, and the money is no longer enough to compensate for the lack of fulfilment. Or maybe you have not stayed loyal to one firm or career at all; instead you have drifted from job to job without any clear sense of long-term goals, and now in mid-life you feel you want to take charge of your own destiny for the first time.

Well, maybe you failed to recognize yourself here – the types are clichés and there are plenty of other categories we could have chosen in their stead. But these illustrations do help us to draw together some common themes. None of these people has access to a large amount of capital, and for various reasons they have come to believe that the way to self-fulfilment and/or financial success lies through self-employment, perhaps leading in due course to a full-scale small business in which others may also be employed.

Assessing yourself

Take stock for a moment. Is setting up a business really appropriate for you? What are your motives? If you are unemployed you may be looking for a degree of financial security, at least in the medium term; you may feel that even if you were lucky enough to secure another conventional job with an established local employer, there would be no guarantee that you would not lose your job again within a year or two because of the precarious nature of the local economy. So perhaps you have decided that you would rather take responsibility for your own success or failure, and stand or fall by your own efforts.

But have you really considered the risks? Even if you are not planning to borrow large sums of money, or to put your house on the line as security for a loan, there is bound to be some financial loss if the business goes under. Have you discussed the possibility of failure with your family? While it is important not to be defeatist, it is also prudent to cater for all eventualities, and to work out exactly how much you could afford to lose if the worst came to the worst. Give yourself a realistic time limit in which to achieve realistic targets. Later we will be discussing in more detail the need for a cash-flow forecast to cover the first year of trading, but right from the outset you need to work out how much *you* will need to be drawing in order to live while you are building up that client/customer base.

If you see your conventional employment as unfulfilling, a creative impulse may be more important to you than the financial question. This may depend on the kind of employment you were previously involved in. An example: perhaps you were working in a large laboratory, part of a factory, and were dissatisfied with the way your career was progressing; there appeared to be no relationship between ability and effort in yourself, and progress up the company ladder. Money may not be the primary consideration here, but it might be if you worked for a smaller firm, had had more of an influence over the direction of that firm, but had faced the disadvantage of a lower wage due to the relative lack of success of the company. Even if you are fed up with your existing job, the reaction of most people in this situation would be to start applying for another one rather than determining to go it alone. You may be increasingly dissatisfied, but in many cases a business will not emerge as a reality until you are made redundant.

Do think carefully about whether your character is suited to going it alone. You may have spent years behind a desk in a busy office or among friends on the shop floor – will you be able to cope with being completely on your own at work for the first time? This is not just a question of your own well-being: the self-discipline required to work unsupervised for any length of time is very considerable and often underestimated by those who have not yet had to face this situation. It may be that you would be happier in partnership with a colleague whose skills and enthusiasm would complement your own, though finding such a paragon might not be easy.

If, on the other hand, you are simply the kind of person who resents being given orders, however sensible or courteous, and who simply cannot settle down as an employee, then you will presumably have given some thought to this question of self-discipline already (you may of course just be the kind of person who hates work, but in that case ask yourself whether you should be reading this book at all). You too will have to consider very carefully whether your independence of spirit might lead to hot-headedness if unchecked, and whether it might not be better to be in a more balanced partnership. After all, your attitude to an important customer or client might sometimes have to be rather like that of a worker to his employer – you simply cannot afford to be rude, however much you disagree with the person. Punctuality is important, for example; if you fail to turn up when expected, you will drive your potential customers mad.

Here are the kinds of questions you should be asking yourself:

- Am I self-disciplined, or do I tend to let things drift?
- Would I be working completely on my own?
- Have I got enough money to live on if times are hard?
- Am I enthusiastic about working as hard as necessary for my own rewards?

- Am I enthusiastic about taking my own decisions?
- Am I happy to cope with the boring paperwork as well as meeting the customers?
- Can I cope under stress?
- Can I take advice, and learn from my mistakes?
- Am I patient and able to plan for long-term development?
- Do I have the full support of my family?

The last point is a very important one. You may of course find that the terrific moral support provided by members of your family compensates for the feeling of being on your own. On the other hand, there will be hard times, no matter how successful you are – every business has its up and down periods and it may be some time before you learn to spot these coming. You must be prepared to live with the insecurity; the absence of a regular weekly or monthly pay cheque is perhaps the most difficult thing to adjust to in the early days of your own business.

Some of these questions may seem difficult to relate to in concrete terms. Try to recall previous episodes, not necessarily part of your work, which have involved this sort of problem. For example, if you are the kind of person who fixes the leak in the roof as soon as it occurs, either by doing it yourself or getting estimates from builders, that may be a positive sign. If you have an old desk upstairs in which bank and credit card statements, paid and unpaid bills, letters and press cuttings jostle together for space in what you regard as delightful chaos, that might suggest a lack of attention to accounting which could land you in trouble as a business person.

None of these individual attributes are to be regarded as conclusive indicators – if you really are incapable of organizing yourself financially, you could pay somebody to sort out your office systems for you. The point of the exercise is rather to address the realities which you will face daily in business and to ask yourself some hard questions about your ability to cope. Some of these realities will be easier for you than others; you will have to weigh up the contradictory answers and try to paint a rounded picture of yourself. If you still find the exercise impossible, or if the results seem hopelessly inconclusive, ask your family and your friends what they think by all means, but do please impress on them the need to be honest and even critical. If they really do think you would be hopeless at organizing your own time, getting on with your customers, or understanding the importance of keeping proper records, it really is better that they should tell you now.

Once you have thought carefully about the risks as well as the rewards of running a business, of taking full responsibility for your own work, you will need to start thinking about what kind of business you plan to run. This too will involve some realistic self-assessment. There is no need to be frightened of the concept: self-assessment can even be fun. All it means is that you will need to take a long, hard and, hopefully, objective look at yourself, at the work you have done and the skills and qualifications you have developed. Look also at your leisure interests and your enthusiasms: you will have acquired knowledge and developed skills in pursuing these as well, and they too might enable you to make a living, something which might not have occurred to you up to now.

First, list any formal qualifications you may have: GCEs or CSEs or even GCSEs, degrees, professional qualifications (e.g. membership of the Institute of Personnel Management), City and Guilds, HNDs – whatever you have, put it down. Indeed, put it down even if you studied for it in vain; the study alone will have given you some knowledge of the field, which you may be able to use. Formal qualifications like these *are* important: if you intend to use the knowledge you have acquired directly in the business venture, they can give potential clients confidence in your ability to do the job; they also suggest that you may be capable of further study to acquire new qualifications in another field. But they are only one factor to be taken into consideration in the overall self-assessment; to give too much emphasis to them is a mistake.

Now note skills you acquired or courses you attended while in employment with somebody else – perhaps you served an apprenticeship as a bricklayer or an electrician, for example. Remember, these work experiences do not have to be things you enjoyed doing at the time. The point is to look for skills which could be applied in other situations, rather than to assume that you will have to work as a bricklayer because laying bricks is the only thing you know. It might be that you want to continue in the same line of work, of course, but it does not have to be like that.

Make a list of things you enjoy doing, leisure activities you spend a significant amount of time on. Perhaps you enjoy buying and doing up old furniture (or old houses); maybe you like nothing better than to get stuck into a major DIY project, such as installing a fitted kitchen; or perhaps you spend all your time maintaining your Triumph Stag, or playing with your personal computer. Be realistic about the amount of time you spend in pursuit of each of these activities, and above all about your level of expertise. What is likely, though, is that you will be too modest, that you will lack the confidence to describe yourself as an expert in something you regard as a mere leisure activity. Get a friend who knows a bit about the subject to assess you here, to give his or her impressions of where your main interests and skills lie. And write it all down.

Remember also to write down details of any clubs or societies you belong to in connection with these interests, or indeed with your employment. If you are looking for a partner with an interest in the same sort of business, these could be very valuable. They could also serve as networks of information on your chosen field of operation. And of course they are fertile ground for wider business contacts and even potential customers. That does not mean you have to bore all your friends silly pressing your business cards into the hands of everyone you meet, but the fact remains that if you are in business for yourself you make your own opportunities and you must be able to make the most of any which do crop up in social situations. Apart from the fact that potential customers may have confidence in you as a businessman simply because they know you already, you are also usually talking to people when they are relaxing and in a good mood. It does help.

The importance of treating your leisure activities as seriously as your employment record should not be underestimated. Setting up in business is not going to be easy, and you need to sustain your morale in the ups and downs which will inevitably mark the early days. Because of this, it is vital that you are enthusiastic about what you are doing, that you believe in the service or product you are offering, that you enjoy the work itself and not just the money-making role it holds in your life. Of course, it may be that you loved working as a bricklayer or a personnel manager, and you want to continue to do the same kind of work on a self-employed basis. Fine. But equally, it may be that one of the reasons why you wanted to set up in business was because you were not enjoying your previous job enough. And that may have been as much because of the nature of the work itself as the firm or organization you worked for. So think very carefully about it.

There is no need to be worried by a change of career, and certainly no need to think of your first career as a failure if you do want to try something completely different – after all, few people exercise much real choice over the work they choose at sixteen, eighteen or whatever. All too often we allow ourselves to be pushed by parents, teachers, financial circumstances, or just lack of anything else immediately available, into a job which might not have been at all what we would have chosen had we genuinely been able to sit down and think carefully about our own future. Setting up in business does give you an opportunity to exercise a real choice over what you want to do. Use it.

Your business idea

While you are still thinking about precisely what service or product you propose to market to the public, the leisure or social activities we have been discussing are valuable in a quite different, much more passive, way. In short, you need to listen to people talking; if possible, steer the conversation in the direction of your neighbourhood (town, suburb, group of villages or whatever) and its drawbacks. It is never difficult to get people to grumble; while you listen you are gaining valuable feedback about possible business opportunities in the locality. Young mothers will moan about the shortage of childminders or playgroups, or even nannies (if you're living in yuppie territory). In London and the south-east, where house prices are the staple diet of many a dinner-table or saloon-bar conversation, everybody will complain about the high fees and poor service offered by local estate agents. And of course about the problems of getting a good old-fashioned landscape gardener or craftsman-builder to help with the overgrown lawn or the extension.

If you are interested in providing any kind of personal service, it will probably be at a local level, at least in the early stages. So listen to people. Do not just assume that you have worked out what you are going to do already, and consequently switch off. Anything people say which will help you to provide a more comprehensive service, or to market your service more effectively, should be noted very carefully. Write it down, and let people see you do it. They will probably be flattered to see you taking note of their advice, as well as impressed by your businesslike efficiency.

Pay particular attention if anybody tells you one of these three things:

- That all the local businesses in one of your spheres of interest charge far too much for less than impressive work.
- That these same businesses are oversubscribed, and it is impossible to get anybody to take on smaller jobs.
- That nobody seems to be offering a particular service in the area, and if somebody were, he/she would get lots of work, because everybody says how much they could do with somebody in that line to call on.

Avoid getting too carried away if you do hear somebody saying something like this. The person you bump into in the street may not be a business-minded individual. He or she has no idea of the costs involved in setting up the kind of business they are so expertly talking about, have no idea of any legislation which may be involved, or indeed of how much you would have to charge to make an honest living. If there are no similar businesses operating in the area, this in itself may be rather suspicious – people may have tried already, and met insuperable problems.

So be sceptical. Ask your friendly neighbourhood gossip whether he/she knows whether anybody used to offer the service, but had to close down. If you know the names of any such defunct businesses, and if after your preliminary investigations you are still interested in the idea, you may be able to locate some of these people. This may depend on how tight-knit a community you live in, but if the people are still in the area (perhaps engaged in a totally different kind of business, more successfully) you may be able to make contact. If you find them in a good and prosperous mood, they may volunteer some trade secrets. Hint that you might be able to do business with them – they may still have lists of former clients/customers and good leads which could still be invaluable, assuming they folded within the last three years or so. It is not a sensible idea to offer actual cash for such information or leads – after all, it may turn out to be a completely useless set of names, people who have long since moved or whose business has closed down, or who are now quite happy to use another firm further afield for their needs. But perhaps you could agree to pay a percentage of any business you procure from the defunct business's former customers.

By now you will be getting feedback on the kinds of businesses there might be an indentifiable need for, and you are able to match this information with the self-assessment you carried out earlier. Do not be surprised or worried if there is no obvious match at first sight – if you really do feel that bricklaying is the only thing you can do, but everybody says the only need is for plumbers, this may seem depressing. But there are two options for you here: you could embark on a plumbing course (if you have worked as a bricklayer for some time you will probably often have come into contact with plumbers, and you will in any case be a practically minded person who will be able to pick up at least the basics of a new trade without too much of a struggle). On the other hand, you could look for a partner with plumbing skills – ask around, and you may find there are opportunities for just such a team to build kitchen or bathroom extensions. An extreme example perhaps, but one you may profit from. Avoid being too set on one idea. If you can offer more than one skill – roofing, plumbing, plastering – you will be in a much better position to quote for a whole job, rather than having to stop when the basic building work is done, which is annoying for the householder who then has to find somebody else to do the next stage.

As was noted earlier, there are some trends in the economy which you would do well to take note of, though that does not mean that you cannot make a living from another kind of business which does not fit into one of these areas. In general, your small business is going to be in a stronger position if it is offering the kind of specialist product or service which the giants of the economy simply cannot manage; one of the paradoxes of modern living in Britain is that as mergers and takeovers mean that a smaller number of companies control the lion's share of the economy, at the same time there is an increasing, almost obsessive, demand for the individual, the one-off product which nobody else has got. By definition, such a product cannot be mass-produced, and if you can hit on the right idea, you can win here.

But this is not, of course, only true of products – the trend is just as relevant in the service sector. The growth in specialized consultancy of all kinds is a notable development, but there are also cleaning, catering, teaching or removal services (to take just a few obvious examples) which may be too small for the larger organizations in your area to be able to offer, while being perfectly profitable for the smaller operator with smaller overheads. Some of these, especially in the cleaning field, may be offered as franchises, which may give you the advantage of a big name if the field really is competitive locally. If it is, is it really a sensible market for you? And if it is not, do you need the franchise 'name' to establish yourself? You need to be asking yourself just this kind of question all the time.

What kind of business?

The mention of franchises introduces another area altogether, the whole question of your operation and its structure. What are you going to be: sole trader, partnership, limited company, co-operative, franchise? This is important; look at each possible mode in turn.

The sole trader

Operating as a sole trader is the easiest thing to do, and the most likely format for anybody reading this book. If you are a sole trader you are the sole owner of your business, and you can start trading whenever you like without any legal formalities. There are absolutely no legal requirements about the kind of accounts you must keep, although it is obviously very much in your own interest that you do keep a proper record of all income and expenditure. If you do not, the Inland Revenue will assess you for tax at a much higher level than may be necessary, and the onus will then be on you to prove that your income was in fact lower than the figure suggested – you cannot prove that without having full details of your business income and expenditure.

What this does mean, though, is that you do not have to have your accounts audited by a professional accountant every year; provided that you keep your own records very carefully, there should be very little for an accountant to do, though you may still want to employ a professional to complete and submit your tax returns. The only real disadvantage of being a sole trader is that you are personally liable for all your business debts. Whether this is indeed a serious disadvantage will depend partly on how much money you must borrow or find at the outset, and partly on how much credit you are likely to be giving. The whole question of cash flow will be considered later, but in most cases capital requirements of less than £5000 are likely to mean that this form of trading is the most sensible.

One point you will need to consider is the name you will be trading under. If you are offering some kind of consultancy or personal service on a freelance basis, your own name may be perfectly adequate. But if you are at all likely to be employing other people and offering a range of services or products, there are advantages in putting an attractive name on your letterhead and sales literature. So think carefully about it; one aspect you may want to consider is the use of an initial 'key word' associated with the type of business, which may enable people to find you in the alphabetical, and not just the Yellow Pages, section of your local telephone directory. Again, the sole trader has the edge here, because the Registry of Business Names was abolished in 1982, and you can call yourself anything you like within reason; all you must do is display a notice containing the names of the owners of the business, and an address to which legal documents should be served. The local Chamber of Commerce will advise on this.

The partnership

So you have a partner in mind: your wife, lover, best friend, ex-colleague from work, or just that man you met in the pub last night who had all those wonderful ideas. There is not a lot of point in going into a partnership with somebody unless that person can bring additional benefits to the business. It may be worthwhile if he or she has skills which you lack (a bricklayer starting a building business with a joiner is perhaps the classic example). Or it may be that the person has excellent contacts derived from previous employment which could bring both of you a lot of business.

Two words of warning here. First, it is best to have a formal partnership agreement drawn up by a solicitor with plenty of small-business experience. However good your relationship is with your partner, do not forget that when money is involved friendships are not infallible. It is vital that you establish your responsibilities, decide how you draw out income, and arrange what happens if one of you wants to break up the partnership. The relevant section in *Starting your own business – the practical steps*, published by the Small Firms Service, is helpful on the legal points.

Secondly, it is a good principle not to go into a partnership unless it is absolutely essential for the good of the business. In other words, if you can run the business without your partner, why not do so? If he or she brings in specialist knowledge which is required only occasionally, would it not be more sensible to pay for such advice on a freelance basis?

The limited company

Much of what we said about partnerships also applies here, with the exception that limited companies are often a way of raising money for a business venture. It is quite possible to have a director and sole employee, who acts in most respects like a sole trader on a day-to-day basis, but who is also responsible to three or four other directors, none actively involved in the business, but all representing individual or institutional shareholders. It is unlikely that anybody wanting to borrow as little as £5000 would be interested in this kind of set-up, but it is worth pointing out the advantages and pitfalls.

The obvious advantage, though it may sound rather defeatist, is that in the event of bankruptcy no individual director is personally liable for the debts of the company, but only for the amount he or she has formally invested in the business. However, in the case of bank loans this is largely meaningless, since a bank will almost certainly demand some kind of personal guarantee. There are also tax advantages in being a company once you start to generate large profits, but this is not something to concern yourself with yet. Similarly, limited companies may just be able to obtain more favourable terms and service from suppliers, though this is unlikely to make a great deal of difference at the outset.

Limited companies must present accounts annually to Companies

House in a form laid down by successive Companies Acts, and these accounts must have been audited (i.e. checked) by a qualified chartered or certified accountant. This audit obviously costs money, and the deposited accounts are open to public inspection – so any rival firm can obtain details of the turnover and expenditure of your company in past years. Another minor disadvantage is that working directors of limited companies are employees, taxed through the PAYE system and therefore unable to take advantage of the self-employed tax assessment rules. Even if you and your spouse are the only directors of your company, you are still not self-employed in the technical sense.

If you do want to set up a limited company, you will certainly need legal help with the registration – for example, you are not allowed to use the name of another existing company. Again, a good solicitor with plenty of small-business experience is the person to discuss things with.

The co-operative

This is one for the idealists, and not to be considered unless you are one of a group committed to the ideal. Usually the group comes together to pool skills and resources; ideally participants are aware of each others' strengths and weaknesses through prior experience at school or college, in work, or through leisure pursuits. The fundamental principle is of democratic control by the workforce, each member holding an equal share in the enterprise and an equal responsibility for its success or failure; it is usual for co-operative enterprises to acquire limited company status. The chief benefits are of real involvement in the direction of the business, leading to a greater commitment on the part of the workforce in terms of both time and money, and greater personal reward.

All that has been said about the problems of partnership applies to an even greater extent here, and no co-operative can afford to neglect basic business principles of selling in a competitive market. There may also be problems in raising start-up capital. Before launching into this kind of venture it is essential that you and your group seek out the experts: the Co-Operative Development Agency produce a range of excellent publications and will provide local contacts throughout Britain; the Leeds-based Industrial Common Ownership Movement is also worth seeking out.

The franchise

The British Franchise Association provides the following definition:

> Franchising is the method by which the owner of a business [franchisor] contractually agrees to allow another independent person, or company [franchisee] to market its product or service within a specified geographical area. In return, the franchisee pays an initial fee for the rights to the area and a royalty on sales giving the franchisor a percentage benefit on sales.

Many people think a franchise offers the ideal sure-fire business success. Not so. There are indeed some very well-known and successful franchises: Wimpy, British School of Motoring, Kall-Kwik. But just because a company has a famous name does not mean that all of its franchised outlets meet with similar success. And in any case, such famous names are not likely to be of much interest to those with less than £5000 to invest.

Helpfully, the British Franchise Association goes on to make a distinction between three different types of franchise, only the first of which need concern you, in the context of a £5000 capital limit. This is the Job Franchise, typically a service like car tuning or carpet cleaning; the franchisee is taught the skill required, invests in necessary equipment and then earns money based on the number of hours he or she works.

Job franchises will require relatively little start-up capital, then. But the crucial question to ask is: do you really need the franchise at all? Why not go on a cleaning or engine-tuning course, buy some secondhand equipment, and set up shop with the benefit of some cheap local advertising? Ultimately you are going to have to decide whether a much-vaunted national name and image, and some help with legal and financial matters which you could probably get easily enough anyway, is worth your initial fee and percentage on turnover.

Do bear in mind that such franchises will pass on marketing costs to the consumer; from the consumer's point of view they will almost certainly be more expensive than rival sole traders. Because of this, you may have an uphill struggle unless you can convince people that the franchise advertising really means something and that they are getting something unique for their money, or alternatively you are engaged in a highly specialized field with few if any competitors. Consumers are increasingly sophisticated; they know to shop around. Should you not be just as sophisticated in deciding whether to operate as a franchise or to go it alone? Remember that if you are a franchisee, you will be very restricted in the way you choose to run the business, and if your primary urge to set up in business is the creative one, this could be a very significant disadvantage.

This is perhaps to emphasize the negative aspects of franchising too much; the BFA claims that the 'established' franchises – the genuine ones it is keen to promote – have a success rate as high as 90 per cent. If you are interested, do contact the BFA, who will supply a list of their members, and who also organize exhibitions from time to time, in which visitors have an opportunity to meet representatives from a wide variety of businesses and discuss things in more detail. The Association tries to uphold high ethical standards, and only allows into membership tried and tested businesses; their definition is a pilot scheme operated successfully for at least a year, and evidence of successful franchising with at least four franchisees over a subsequent two-year period. But do bear in mind that many quite genuine franchises, including some of the most successful names, are not members of the Association. In these circumstances all the Association can do is provide advice on the questions you should be asking.

One final point. The secretary of the BFA was quoted in June 1988 as saying that most of the problems brought to their attention were at the lower end of the market, and that there were few genuine opportunities available for under £10,000. To some extent you get what you pay for.

Sources of advice

This area has already been touched on in the discussion on different types of businesses – bodies such as the Co-Operative Development Agency and the British Franchise Association are certainly sources of advice which nobody concerned with their particular spheres of interest should ignore. But what about the broader range of bodies – some funded by national or local government; some with private backing – with aims that include help to men and women wanting to start their own businesses? Most people would agree that there is at least a greater willingness to talk about support for small businesses these days. So how far does the talk get carried into practice? What are likely to be the bodies first on the list of the budding small-business person, and what kind of help do they offer?

The Small Firms Service

If you dial 100 and ask the operator for Freefone Enterprise, you will be connected to your nearest Small Firms Centre, one of a network of thirteen throughout Great Britain. Their computer-based information service is the one to go for if you have specific questions about business problems, but perhaps not so useful for the person entirely new to the business field. However, a Centre will put you in touch with contacts in other local agencies and authorities, and does offer a business counselling service (three free sessions); again, this may be more useful to a person whose business is already established and who is experiencing the different kinds of problem which go with expansion into new markets. While you are on the telephone, you might as well get the Small Firms Service to send you copies of their free booklets, covering such topics as Accounting and Marketing. The style of some of these is legalistic rather than inspirational, but they may help with matters of fact.

The 1987–8 annual report of the Small Firms Service does illustrate the growth in this sector of the economy: a 50 per cent increase in self-employment between 1980 and 1987, for example. The SFS has set up a Centre for European Business in preparation for the 1992 Single Market, and another new development is that the SFS database is now sold to local enterprise agencies and organizations advising small firms. In general, the Small Firms Centres like to see themselves as the gateways to all other forms of assistance, a first port of call for those unsure where to turn.

Local Enterprise Agencies

These are local organizations working with national and local authorities towards establishing business initiatives in their local area; the Small Firms Centres will give details of the ones nearest to you. This is important because they are not always called Enterprise Agencies; those run under the auspices of Labour councils, for example, tend to be known as the Employment Development or Economic Development Unit. Local Enterprise Agencies are dotted throughout the country, and the services they offer vary, but they will all be prepared to give free advice on starting up, book-keeping, marketing, and so on. They will also know about training courses operating in the area, and the larger ones are themselves actively involved in organizing such courses, which often operate a vetting procedure to make sure that all participants are genuinely committed to the idea of their own enterprise. This may sound unpleasant, but is in fact an advantage, since it helps potential business people to think through their ideas in advance so that they make maximum use of the limited training time available.

Special mention should be made of the London Enterprise Agency (LEntA), which is funded by seventeen large companies to help small businesses and job creation. It offers, for example, one day Introductory Courses on particular types of business such as hairdressing or catering, as well as a more advanced seven-day grounding in business skills; an Export Enterprise Programme for small businesses looking to develop into overseas markets; a 'Marriage Bureau' to link small businesses seeking capital and management help with those wishing to invest and work in such firms; and help with finding premises, including a free list of small managed workshop space in London.

The Rural Development Commission

Formerly the Council for Small Industries in Rural Areas, the Commission produces an excellent and very attractive booklet *Action for Rural Enterprise* which should be obtained at the outset by anybody wanting to set up in a market town or rural area of England. The booklet is divided into sections highlighting resources (such as premises, finance, and training), and then different types of business (such as tourism and leisure, organic farming, and transport). Each section gives an outline of further assistance which may be available and a checklist of which organizations to approach – would you have thought of English Heritage, water authorities or the Business Services Department of the National Farmers' Union? A model of what a government publication should be.

The RDC's Business Service in each rural county of England will also provide free business and technical advice for anybody in a town of fewer than 10,000 inhabitants, runs training courses, and sells technical publications on subjects as diverse as thatching or furniture design. Grants are not generally available for rural businesses, but in the 28 Rural Development Areas, grants can cover the cost of converting redundant buildings into workshops. The Business Service in 1988 had a total of 32,700 firms on its books, a 20 per cent increase over the previous year and nearly double the 1983/4 figure.

Citizens' Advice Bureaux

These admirable, though nowadays overworked, organizations will be of particular help to locally based businesses with specific problems; for example, they may be able to put you in touch with a reputable accountant, they will certainly give general advice on any legal requirements which exist for the kind of business you want to run, and they will also help if you do need to register your business with the local council and need advice on how to do it.

The Enterprise Allowance Scheme

The EAS, run by the Manpower Services Commission, is not merely a source of advice: its importance is so great to so many that it must be examined in depth. It celebrated its fifth birthday in 1988, and government figures proclaim a great success story: 65 per cent of participants still trading after three years; each, on average, creating an extra job. There has been much debate about whether the Scheme really is increasing the level of self-employment; an alternative view is that in most of the obvious fields of endeavour, such as hairdressing, each successful new business simply forces a longer-established venture to cease trading, there being only so much employment for hairdressers in any one locality. But the debate is not really relevant to the present discussion, although it may be worth bearing in mind that there is indeed likely to be more competition from existing businesses in some of the more obvious types of services or products; unless you really are offering something better, it might be as well to consider doing something more specialized.

The broad advantages of the Scheme are quite well known: a grant of £40 per week for the first year of trading, together with free business advice. If you inquire at your local Jobcentre, you will be told in general terms about the Scheme and asked whether you would like to be booked in to an 'Awareness Day', probably at a local college – there is no other way of obtaining an Application Form. The Day starts at 9.30; typically there will be 20–30 participants, who might range from redundant executives with leather briefcases to school-leavers with punk hairstyles. Some will already have done a great deal of preparation work for their businesses, others almost nothing, which dictates the nature of the proceedings (what might be termed the lowest-common-denominator principle).

In future each person applying to go on the Scheme will be required to produce a business plan (see Chapter 2), and the nature of the Awareness Day is now geared to this. There are helpful handouts on cash-flow forecasts and costing, for example, though the session on marketing must inevitably be too generalized to be of much help. There is often no opportunity to become involved except by asking questions at the end of each session, and no time to discuss individual projects except in private conversation during breaks. If, like many participants, you have already gone into the business plan question in some depth – on a course or whatever – you may regard the day as little more than an obstacle to be sat through to earn the precious application form.

As an illustration of this, most interest tends to be shown in the opening talk by an EAS representative on the rules of the scheme. There are few restrictions on the nature of the enterprise itself; essentially, the government is not prepared to fund anything with which it might not like to be associated: politics, religion, gambling, sex or the occult. You cannot work more than eight hours per week for somebody else, and you have to have £1000 available in a bank account as evidence of serious intent, though this is not likely to be a major problem for anybody with a sound proposal. More important, you must have been unemployed and in receipt of benefit for eight weeks prior to your application, and this rule cannot be broken. On the day they receive your application, the EAS staff will telephone your benefit office to check you out; if you are not currently in receipt of benefit, your application will be instantly rejected. The administrators of the Scheme are only interested in funding businesses which otherwise would not get off the ground, and it is as well to be aware of this. If you are interested in applying for the Scheme, you must not sign off until after your application has been approved.

You cannot enter into contracts for the supply of goods or services before the start date approved by the scheme, but there *are* things you can do in advance and while still claiming benefit: find premises and apply for planning permission, obtain a licence to operate, get quotes from suppliers, carry out market research, and contact potential customers to establish demand. The main thing about the EAS is that you must look into it well before you plan to start trading. Get a copy of the rules from your Jobcentre, and make sure you retain your entitlement.

These are only a very few of the most obvious areas of help, but these bodies will direct you to the more specialized sources of advice and information appropriate to your particular needs. Nor should you neglect other literature or TV programmes, often put out regionally: the excellent HTV series *You're the Boss* which went out in the summer of 1988 is a case in point. The National Extension College produces a range of valuable material: its *Be Your Own Boss Starter Kit* is a best-seller widely used by Enterprise Agencies, with a follow-up *Be Your Own Boss Growth Kit* suitable for small businesses which have survived the first year. Uniquely, the College publishes books aimed at people for whom English is a second language starting up a business in this country. The books accompanied the BBC television series *Talking Business* and are available in eight languages.

One other very obvious group of institutions to call on is the High Street banks, several of which publish their own small-business handbooks. But these deserve a section to themselves in the next chapter; in any case, you are not ready for them yet.

2

YOUR BUSINESS PLAN

What is a business plan?

The business plan is about far more than raising capital; it is the next stage you must go through after you have looked at yourself and your situation, after you have come up with your business idea. Indeed, it can be said that the self-assessment and market research you have been doing in the previous chapter has been the preparation for the business plan.

So what exactly is a business plan? Is it just a posh phrase for going to see the bank manager and asking nicely for an overdraft? It is helpful to see it as made up of four components; unless your plan encompasses each of these four, it is not going to add up, it is not going to impress anybody and it is not going to work.

1. You

This is where your self-assessment comes in. What is your educational and employment background? What are your leisure enthusiasms and how do they fit into your business idea? What are the skills and characteristics which will enable you to run not just a successful small business, but *this* successful small business? And in financial terms, what is your personal survival budget, the minimum amount of money you must take out of your business in order to live without hardship?

2. Your resources

Do you intend to work from home, or will you need office and/or storage facilities? Do you need a separate business telephone line, an answering machine, a typewriter or word processor, a fax machine, a desk and filing cabinet? What are your printing needs: letterhead, invoices, business cards, compliments slips? Will you need legal or financial advice? What about stock or parts? Specialist equipment (e.g. for carpet cleaning)? Extra personnel? How much are these fixed costs (or overheads) going to amount to?

3. Your market

What makes you think your idea is a winner? What evidence do you have that people in your neighbourhood will pay what you say they will for the service or product you want to provide? Is there any local competition? If so, what do your competitors charge and how do their services/products differ from what you are looking to provide? How do you intend to reach your market: by newspaper advertising, direct mail, leaflet drops, telephone selling? How much will all this cost, how much will you sell, and how much do you need to sell?

4. Your money

This is where it all comes together. You know your market and how to reach it, you know what equipment and facilities you need to help you get there, you know what you have to spend to live. Now you have to work out totals. And you have to work out what your earnings will be from month to month, so that you can monitor your cash flow.

In all of this you must not lose sight of your overall objective. This will vary from business to business and from individual to individual; it is likely to involve impressing the bank manager enough for him or her to back you by offering an overdraft of up to £5000 for an agreed period. Your task is to demonstrate clearly just how much you need to borrow and why; and how you propose to pay that loan back, and when. It is not just a question of the figures adding up (though add up they must): you also have to show that you are capable of running the business, and that the business you have earmarked is a potentially profitable one.

What if you already have the capital you need to get started? Perhaps you think you need not bother with this section of the book. Think again. The business plan is not a game. There is a wide degree of consensus about what should be in it, not because bank managers like their business plans to conform to a set pattern, but because the structure the plan offers is the best way of assessing the viability of a particular business idea, as projected by a particular individual or group. The plan is meant for you as much as for the bank manager; indeed, it is more use to you because it should be a constant source of reference, to be revised and updated in the light of your actual business experience.

A plan requires discipline and it requires commitment, the very kind of discipline and commitment you are going to need again and again if you are going to run a successful business. It is a surprisingly demanding task to actually sit down and detail your objectives and strategy, on a short- and long-term basis, to decide whether you are interested in sticking to a small specialized business or whether you have broader plans for future expansion, to work out your potential profitability and capital requirements. Many people cop out: they claim to be dealing with such a small, unique or complex business which they know so well that a business plan is a waste of time when they could be out generating work. Ignore the business plan at your peril.

Your personal survival budget

So how do you start? You have done your market research, you have assessed yourself, you are ready to go. What next? When it comes to figures, most people are familiar with their everyday needs and expenses; why not start with your personal survival budget, which you may prefer to call 'drawings' if you dislike the idea of sounding a bit like the victim of a nuclear holocaust. This is easiest if you draw up a chart (see p. 37): a list of items in one column, a figure in pounds in the other. Whether you express this figure in weekly, monthly or yearly terms does not matter much at this stage, as long as each item of expenditure is expressed in terms of the same period. So decide at the outset which period you will use; it may be governed by such matters as whether you pay rent weekly or a mortgage repayment monthly. Just use whatever system is easiest for you.

As you consider each item, you will need to remember two things. The first is that the figures will not in most cases be fixed; what you are paying now will not necessarily be what you will pay in six or nine months' time. So be cautious: added on at least 10 per cent to each figure to give yourself plenty of room for manoeuvre. And round the figures up to the nearest multiple of five or ten; nobody is going to want to see insignificant items listed. So please, no pence. If your monthly mortgage repayment is currently £361.17, put it down as £400.

The other (perhaps obvious) point is that the list in the example is not intended to be exhaustive, but merely to give you the general idea of what is required and get you started. You may have other regular expenses: deliveries from a wine society or book club, vet's fees for your elderly and sick spaniel, alimony to your ex-spouse. Similarly, some of the items listed may not apply to you – you may not have children or run a car. Use your common sense and try to include any regular expenses which add up to a significant amount over a period of time. You might spend an evening looking through your cheque stubs and bills for a period of three or four months just to see exactly where the money went and to make sure nothing major has been left out.

Most of the items will be self-explanatory, but do remember that the figures for telephone, electricity and so on refer only to your personal expenditure outside the business. If you are going to work from home, you will eventually have to apportion business and personal expenditure from your total bill for electricity; for the same reason, it may be a good idea to install a separate business telephone line. At this stage you are not concerned with that, but you must make sure you are not including estimates for business expenditure in your personal survival budget by mistake.

Do not feel embarrassed about jotting down figures for holidays or trips to the theatre or the occasional meal out. Although we have termed the exercise a personal survival budget, the aim is to calculate how much you need to live on, not just to survive. If you allow for no means of relaxation, no money for holidays or other outings, you are unlikely to be giving your best. And even if you are, your bank manager is likely to look a trifle askance at a business which can only achieve profitability if its owner exists on starvation rations and works a sixteen-hour day. The key to the business plan is realism; you are trying to provide a sober assessment of what your business ought to be capable of achieving, given realistic criteria. One of those criteria is your own standard of living. There may indeed come a time when because of temporary cash-flow problems or bad debts you decide to reduce your own drawings from the business for a limited period. But that comes later; for now your intention is to demonstrate, to yourself as much as to anybody else, that your business is capable of providing you with a decent living.

You will notice that the example includes figures for miscellaneous expenditure and for contingencies. How much you put in here will depend to a degree on the make-up of your list of items; for example, if you only go out for a meal or to the cinema every six months, you may want to include these items here rather than separately. It is more difficult to give advice on a contingency budget; so much depends on the nature of the contingency. But you only have to think of the possibilities – a leaky roof, a failed MOT, a private hip replacement for your mother – to realize that you have to be prepared for the worst. Think perhaps in terms of 10 per cent of your total expenditure; this may be a purely arbitrary figure, but you can console yourself with the thought that the bank manager will be impressed with your foresight.

Assuming that your intention is to be self-employed, rather than an employee of a limited company, you must pay Class 2 National Insurance contributions, either by direct debit or weekly stamp. For the year 1989/90 the contribution was £4.25 per week, so think in terms of £5 to be safe. You may also have to pay Class 4 contributions if your earnings rise above a certain level, but no figure for this can be included at this stage, for obvious reasons.

You now have an overall weekly or monthly or yearly figure which you believe you can live on without undue hardship, but without undue extravagance either. What other income can you now set against this? If you have a pension, or income from investments, or from a house you own and let, put it down. If your spouse or cohabitee has a steady income, and this is likely to continue for the foreseeable future, put that down too.

Apart from being a first stage in assessing the viability of your business idea, drawing up a personal survival budget is a useful exercise in coming to terms with the figures aspect of working for yourself. It also enables you to assess your current lifestyle and decide what is really important to you and which ways of spending money may be less important to you in the future. Remember the first chapter – starting in business for yourself is not just an exercise in money-

PERSONAL SURVIVAL BUDGET

	£ (Monthly)
Rent/mortgage repayment	
Community charge (Poll tax)	
Water	
Electricity	
Gas/oil	
Telephone	
Insurance	
Food	
Clothing	
Car tax and insurance	
Car running expenses	
Car maintenance	
Travel	
Newspapers	
Subscriptions	
Television	
Hire purchase etc.	
Holidays	
Meals out/entertainment etc.	
Children's pocket money etc.	
Christmas/birthdays	
Class 2 NI	
Miscellaneous	
Contingencies	
TOTAL	£
Less: Other income	
SURVIVAL INCOME	£

INITIAL BUSINESS COSTS

Needs	*Value of existing assets (£s)*	*Costs you must find (£s)*
Vehicle		
Vehicle tax etc		
Machinery		
Tools		
Furniture		
Rent/Leases		
Insurance		
Legal fees etc		
Advertising		
Stationery etc		
Telephone		
Equipment maintenance		
Subscriptions		
Materials/stock		
Other costs		
TOTAL (£s)		

making or changing your employer; it represents a fantastic opportunity to take control of your own life, to change direction fundamentally, to do some of the things you always wanted to do but never quite got round to. If you drink or smoke too much, why not use this as an opportunity to cut down, to improve your health and your bank balance at the same time?

Your personal survival budget will not appear in the final version of the plan, except as a single drawings figure. But do not underestimate its importance. Ultimately in business a lender is backing people, and in this case this means you. Unless you are happy with the business and what you can get out of it, there is little point in proceeding.

Your fixed costs

The next step is to work out your initial business costs. Most of the same principles apply – overestimate wherever possible, round up the figures, be realistic about what you need. Again, the illustration will help to set you thinking, but here more than ever your particular business idea will have its own built-in costs. Here too some more complex accounting principles will have to be introduced: assets, value, depreciation. Look at the most obvious example. It is likely that you will need some form of motor transport in operating your business. You might not be worried by this, thinking that you have a perfectly serviceable old banger at home, which will do for a bit. Well, maybe. But leaving aside for a moment the question of whether your family saloon with its baby seat is really suitable for business, what happens when it finally packs up, or when it becomes too expensive to run any more? You need a realistic assessment of its current value and its life expectancy. If your car is worth £1000, and you reckon it has four years of useful life remaining, its value should be decreased by £250 per year, so that in the fourth year it has been reduced to nil, and you are not pretending you still have a valuable asset. Of course, you may find that the machine is still working perfectly after four years, in which case any extra life you get out of it is a bonus. But always be prepared for a realistic level of depreciation.

This depreciation, which represents a £250 reduction in value in the example, is really an expense, one of the running costs of the business. To put it at its simplest, if your motor vehicle is depreciating in value by £250 every year, you should be putting aside £250 so that when the four years are up and the vehicle is no more, you have £1000 to buy another old banger. If you do not do this, if you are the kind of business person who lives entirely for the present, spending all the money you earn and letting the future look after itself, then you might be very lucky and stay in business. It is far more likely that the first large and unexpected bill will force you to cease trading. Be warned.

This depreciation principle must apply not only to vehicles but to any expensive equipment you need for the business which you will need to replace when it no longer works; it should even apply to smaller items like typewriters. What this means is that such items are more expensive than you might otherwise think. The cost of owning a typewriter, a car or a steam cleaner does not end when you buy it, even if you pay cash in full. You have the depreciation to think about, but you also have to remember service charges – perhaps £50 per annum for a service contract on a good electric typewriter. In the case of a vehicle, you have to pay your tax and insurance. So think carefully before you buy anything of this nature. You may need a typewriter, a car, even a small desktop copying machine, if you deal with a lot of paperwork. But do you really need that computer/word processor you have set your heart on? You may imagine yourself seated at a smart new desk in a smart new office on the smart side of town; ask yourself whether you are just playing at business, or whether you want to be serious. If the major part of your work consists of writing – books, articles, reports or whatever – you may well need a word processor. Otherwise, forget the new technology until it will really save your business money and not just boost your personal image.

Many of the other categories are difficult to generalize about, and people may give you contradictory advice. By all means work from home if you have space there. It may be a spare bedroom, it may be a converted garage or even a garden shed, but you must have an area of your property to be used primarily for business purposes and preferably out of bounds for other members of the family, especially during business hours. One of the worst things about working from home is that friends and relatives fail to see it as work at all – they cheerfully ring up to tell you all their woes, or drop in because they think you must be lonely. The minutes turn into hours of lost time, and you find it awkward to turn the visitors away or put the telephone down; worse, you start to enjoy it. It is for this reason, if no other, that you should certainly have a business telephone line installed; it is not really very expensive, and you can then insist on giving the number only to your business acquaintances. An answering machine is also a good investment if you are out of the office much, and have no back-up staff. Nobody likes using them, but people will leave a message if they are really keen to get hold of you, and at the very least it creates a better impression than an unanswered telephone; customers and potential customers are reassured that they have the correct number, and that you are still in business.

Your local authority is unlikely to be bothered about a business operating from a residential address, unless you are in the kind of business which has to be licensed anyway, or employ several staff and have a stream of customers and suppliers blocking everyone's driveway all the time. Depending on how friendly your neighbours are, the council is unlikely even to be aware of the business use, and it is not necessary for you to tell them. Apply for planning permission if they ask you to; it should be a formality unless you are generating complaints from neighbours or the police. As a general rule, try running your business from home if it is in the mail order field, or if you visit your clients or customers at their own premises; otherwise, think in terms of a separate office or workshop.

Supposing your home is unsuitable, and you really have to have business premises from the outset; what should you do? The short answer is: do not buy or enter into long-term agreements. Far better is a short-term agreement to rent an office or warehouse for three months or six months. Your needs may change; your business may change; do not saddle yourself with premises you cannot change. It does make sense to shop around your locality and find out what is available before you finalize your business plan; that way you will be ready to move in as soon as your capital needs have been sorted out. The bank manager will also be more impressed if you can show that you have done your homework, know what you are looking for and where to find it, and show that you are capable of negotiating a simple contract with the minimum of fuss. It is, in effect, your first taste of business and getting what you want.

An already simply furnished office is often a good idea at the outset, as it removes the need for you to spend money on desks, chairs and filing cabinets. Otherwise, try secondhand furniture shops (*not* antique shops). For a smarter look – if you expect to be entertaining clients in your office – there are excellent self-assembly work stations available which may represent everything you need in the early stages and can always be added to later on. Imagine yourself visiting the business for the first time: what would be your impression of the reception area, the lavatories, even the other businesses using the same building? And do not forget to consider parking space and the availability of public transport.

One last word of warning about office rental. Serviced blocks of offices are popular, and the availability of typing, photocopying and fax services may seem ideal. These services are expensive, however, and uneconomic unless you use them only rarely. If you decide to invest in your own copier, you will probably find a clause in your office rental agreement preventing you from importing such machines on to the premises. Unless appearances are important, you may find a dingy room above a shop, where the landlord neither knows nor cares what you do there, to be a better bet. All you really need to make sure of is security, and that you have 24-hour access. But do remember to make sure who pays for rates and electricity; as always the principle is to establish your costs as far as possible in advance. That way you avoid unexpectedly large bills and enjoy the capacity to plan ahead. It may be a good idea to have the agreement checked by a solicitor before you sign, just to maintain peace of mind.

Most of the other categories of initial costs are self-explanatory. It goes without saying that you should get a number of quotes from printers for your stationery needs. Small, independent local printers may well be cheaper than famous name franchises and may well offer a more personal service; against this the big boys will try to entice you in with special offers, packs incorporating letterheads, invoices and business cards for one all-inclusive introductory charge. But the cost is not the only consideration; you will be looking for somebody with a designer's eye, who can help you to choose the right image for your business. Somebody, in short, who knows you and understands what you are trying to achieve.

Do not forget to include business insurance among your overheads. You will of course need to insure your premises and any contents, such as stock. But if you employ anyone, you will also be required to take out employer's liability insurance to cover any injuries employees may suffer in the course of work. And if members of the public use the premises, public liability insurance will be needed for the same reason. As a sole trader, you may want personal sickness and accident insurance to cover you for when you are unable to work. Go and talk to an insurance broker about all these things before you start trading.

Your variable costs

The next part is more difficult. You have to move on from the overheads to a calculation of total yearly expenditure. But how can you possibly know how much headed paper you will use every month? Or how many materials you will have to buy? Surely it will depend entirely on how much you sell, and how will you know how much you will sell until you actually start trading?

So you need to consult your marketing plan. The next chapter,

'Bringing in Business', is concerned primarily with the whole question of how to market your product or service, and you may find it helpful to read that chapter and act on it before you tackle this section of the plan. It is just another illustration of how impossible it is to separate different facets of business life into individual compartments.

How much will you sell in your first year in business? It is fair to say that there is bound to be a certain amount of guesswork here. But you need to be able to provide some evidence to support your figures. One way of doing this is to point to market research you have undertaken in your neighbourhood. To take one very simple example, you may decide there is an obvious shortage of window-cleaners in your locality. Perhaps you carry out a survey of one hundred households, and discover that more than half would be prepared to pay up to £3 to have their windows cleaned once a month. You then assume that fifty households in every hundred will be potential customers; there are 1000 houses on the estate where you live, so that means up to 500 customers, a potential income of £1500 per month. Of course, even if you were able to work at the rate of two houses per hour, a normal working week would only enable you to cope with 80 customers on your own, and there would be no time to cover the whole estate. But the market research you had undertaken would demonstrate that you had identified your potential customers and had a realistic plan of action.

This would be still more impressive if you could point to actual regular contracts in the pipeline. Perhaps you contacted your old school, and asked who did their window-cleaning and how much they charged. If a professional cleaning firm was involved, you should have had no trouble in undercutting and securing an annual contract worth perhaps £500. Similar approaches to other local schools and factories might pay similar dividends and would look very good on your business plan, both as a guarantee of at least some regular income, and as a sign of initiative. You need both to succeed in business. Of course there are disadvantages in regular contract work as well. Until the schools or factories have seen you in action, they may be unwilling to do business with you except on a trial basis; they will also expect you to turn up on the appointed days, whatever the weather, and you will almost certainly have to invest in longer ladders and more sophisticated cleaning equipment. But if your reputation grows, and you secure more contracts from large concerns, you can begin to say goodbye to the door-to-door canvassing for work or even employ younger school-leavers to handle that side of the work for you, taking a profit on their labour as you go. A textbook example of the way a small business could develop.

Perhaps you can now begin to see how you can provide estimated sales figures for your first year of trading. In the window-cleaning example, you bring in a figure of £240 per week, assuming forty hours at £3 per hour. So you write down the figures in monthly columns, starting with your first month of trading, whenever that happens to be, and you end up with a figure of £960 (four weeks at £240). If you are worried about the fact that there are not exactly four weeks in a month, remember that the total of forty-eight working weeks in the year you are accounting for will leave you four weeks for holiday or sickness time, when you will not be paid. It is important that you include time off in your calculations and that you make sure that your bank manager knows you have included it. You may of course want to take all the budgeted time off in one month, or at least in the summer period. If you like you could even plan things in this way, leaving the earnings figure for one month as zero. But that would mean recalculating all the other months to take into account the handful of extra days they included over the basic four weeks. And besides, you cannot really predict when you will want to take your holidays or when you will be ill, and nobody will expect you to; it is enough to demonstrate that you have taken these matters into account. So keep it simple.

It is, however, worth considering whether your business is seasonally based. Even personal services like window-cleaning may need some adjustment; you might be able to work a ten-hour day in the lighter summer months, and only manage an average of six hours in winter when it may be raining or snowing a good deal of the time (whereas of course in summer it never rains in this country!). In the case of a plumber the opposite pattern may emerge: winter will be the time when you work around the clock, answering emergency calls and getting paid handsomely for your service; summer work will be a calmer, bread-and-butter series of jobs. But many other types of business are not so clear-cut: if you are a management consultant or a freelance writer or a textile designer, you ought to be able to market your service all the year round. Again, nobody is going to expect you to know precisely which months will show an upturn or downturn of business; at this stage it is enough to demonstrate your awareness of your market and when it is most likely to buy. Be realistic.

Now you have monthly sales figures you will be able to draw up your variable costs more effectively. In the window-cleaner example these will be negligible; it is unlikely that the householders are going to charge you for water, though you will have to put something aside for soap and cleaning equipment. In the early days you may have to overestimate a bit on this, as you have no means of assessing how much; most people who start window-cleaning businesses are unlikely to have worked for somebody else in the same trade. But for practical purposes you will have overheads and initial capital expenditure (ladders, and possibly transport) rather than variable costs.

Things would be more complicated in a mobile hairdressing business. You certainly will have worked in the trade, probably for a number of years, and you will know how much shampoo and other materials you get through per week on average; you should be able to relate these variable costs to the projected sales figures you have drawn up. On the other hand, if you are visiting your clients in their own homes, you will need a car to get you around, with all the attendant running costs. You are going to be out most of the time, so you will need a business telephone line with an answering machine, so that your clients can ring you to make appointments. All these are overheads. And you will have substantial start-up costs to acquire the tools of the trade; you are most unlikely to have these if you have been working in somebody else's salon.

Whatever your business, there will be some more or less fixed costs;

the rent on an office is the obvious one to point to. But others (like the cost of shampoo, in the example) will be directly related to the number of clients or customers you serve in a given period; you can now begin to see the importance of market research leading to realistic sales figures and in turn a sounder business plan. Variable costs are sometimes called direct costs; this is because they are made up only of expenditure which would not exist if the relevant sales had not been made. Apart from materials and components, the main category will be labour costs, money paid perhaps to part-time workers on a freelance basis whenever sufficient work is available to justify it.

You may feel that other costs will be neither fixed nor entirely customer-led: postage, stationery, advertising are all examples of this problem. You will be spending money initially on your marketing programme, even if no customers appear as a result; on the other hand any sizeable number of customers is going to lead to the use of more stationery (letterhead, invoices, etc) and postage. Nor is it even possible to decide how much you will spend in the first year and list that as a fixed cost, separated from the variable figures for the use of stationery in everyday office life. Your advertising will have to be monitored from day to day and week to week; it varies with the amount of business different forms of advertising bring in, and it will vary as much as anything.

It is a convention of business plans, however, that advertising and stationery costs should be considered as overheads rather than variable; it is just too complicated to split them up. If you are assuming that your level of business will remain static after reaching an initial peak, it will be best to set your marketing costs at a static figure, after spending an initial start-up budget to get the business established. A running figure of 10 per cent of your gross sales income is not unreasonable if you intend to rely mainly on paid advertising, though your bank manager will almost certainly want to know more about how that figure is made up.

Your financial projections

You should now be starting to understand important accounting distinctions: between start-up costs, such as the purchase of a typewriter or machinery, and everyday running costs, such as postage or advertising or office rental; and between overheads and variable costs. The first distinction is vital when you come to draw up your projected profit and loss account and cash-flow forecast for the first year of trading, the two items which will represent the financial core of your business plan and which are the items the bank manager will probably look at first.

The profit and loss account is sometimes known as an income and expenditure account, and you may find it helpful to think of it in these terms. However, it is important to know that certain classes of expenditure are not included in this account; essentially, you do not include the capital start-up costs for equipment, machinery, motor vehicles, etc. This is because they represent unusual one-off payments which should not need to be repeated annually, and which if included would distort the first year's accounts to an unacceptable degree. What you should of course include are the running and maintenance costs associated with such capital items, together with a figure for depreciation. In doing this you will be preparing your business for the time when the equipment needs to be replaced.

It may be helpful to draw up a profit and loss account for, say, three different levels of expectation; in other words you want to show how the profitability of the business varies depending on the level of sales. The example overleaf, drawn from a real business with which the author was associated, shows at the top the total income which would be received from 200, 300 or 400 clients, assuming that each client paid the same all-inclusive fee of £250. Listed below each is the column of expenditure items, once again totalled for the year. Here the second of the two accounting distinctions comes into play: certain charges (advertising, rent, motor expenses) remain unchanged whatever the level of trading; others (printing, postage, fees paid to freelance researchers) increase as the level of sales

PROJECTED PROFIT AND LOSS ACCOUNT (£s)

Number of clients	200	300	400
Income @ £250	50000	75000	100000
EXPENDITURE			
Advertising	10000	10000	10000
Freelance researchers	16667	25000	33333
Salaries & NI	20000	20000	20000
Book-keeping etc	2000	2000	2000
Rent	3000	3000	3000
Motor expenses	2000	2000	2000
Travel	1000	1000	1000
Postage	3000	4500	6000
Printing & stationery	2000	3000	4000
Audit	500	500	500
Bank charges	500	500	500
Equipment maintenance	500	500	500
Sundries	1000	1000	1000
Depreciation	1000	1000	1000
Profit before finance	– 13167	1000	15167
Finance costs	1000	1000	1000
NET PROFIT	– 12167	–	14167

increases, because they are directly related to the number of clients the business needs to service.

Deducting the total expenditure for the year from each of these income figures, we can see what will happen at different levels of trading. In the first set of figures, the level of business constitutes a sizeable loss for the year; in the second (which was felt to be the most realistic target for the year) the business just about breaks even, when anticipated finance costs are taken into account; the third alternative, probably the maximum level of trading the business could cope with given existing resources, demonstrates how the increase in turnover reflects directly in the profitability of the concern, since the overheads have already been covered at a lower level of turnover.

By demonstrating the profitability of your business at different levels of turnover, you will be showing that you have a real grasp of the relationship between income, expenditure and profit; that you understand the difference between fixed costs, or overheads, and variable costs, which increase with the level of sales; that you know what is meant by capital expenditure and why it should play no part in your profit and loss account. Above all, you will have begun to demonstrate that you know how the profitability of a business is not merely a question of having enough money in your bank account.

You will notice that finance costs (i.e. the interest and capital repayments on a loan) have been deducted as a separate item, after an initial profit (or loss) figure has been arrived at. This is standard practice if you have borrowed money from a private individual or company, and might be useful if you have a Business Development Loan from a bank or other financial institution which will be paid back over an agreed period of time, since its purpose was to finance the purchase of specific equipment or otherwise expand the business beyond its current resources. It is quite likely, however, that you will simply need an overdraft facility of £5000 or whatever, from your friendly local bank manager, and that it is your intention that this overdraft facility will continue to be available to you as long as your business needs it, though the bank will expect to see you demonstrate that within two or three years you should not need it any more. In this case there are no regular capital repayments to disturb the profit and loss account, and interest charges can be included as a normal expenditure item. But do make sure that you have done your homework and included figures for this; the bank manager will be less sympathetic if he thinks you expect him to supply you with a free overdraft!

If you have worked out your initial cost figures on a monthly basis, you may well want to put together your projected profit and loss account on that basis too; this will be especially valuable if your work is likely to be seasonal, and it gives you an opportunity to show off the benefits of the research you have done in that direction and impress the bank manager. But do make sure that you have yearly totals as well, which can be referred to at a glance for an overall picture.

Once you have sorted out your costs and drawn up a profit and loss account, it will be a relatively easy matter for you to calculate the break-even point for your business, in other words the precise sales level you will require to cover all those costs. To do this you will need to understand the difference between gross profit and net profit. Gross profit is what you are left with when you take the sales figure and deduct from it all expenses related to those sales – stock and materials being the obvious ones, but also any labour (such as the freelance researchers in our example) which can be directly attributed to the sales you have made. When you have the figure for gross profit, you need to calculate it as a percentage of your sales. This can be expressed simply as follows:

$$\frac{\text{Gross profit}}{\text{Sales}} = \text{gross profit margin}$$

The break-even point for the business in its first year of trading will simply be the total figure for overheads (i.e. all other costs included in the profit and loss account) divided by the gross profit margin you have just worked out. So a gross profit of £30,000 on sales of £100,000 would give you a gross profit margin of 0.33. Divide your overheads figure of £10,000 by this and you will come up with a break-even point at a sales level of £30,000. Of course you are making an assumption here that neither your gross profit margin nor your overheads are going to change much, and the figure you come up with cannot be taken too precisely. But it is useful as an approximate rule of thumb, and important as a monitoring device once you start trading; what you should do is divide the break-even point by twelve to give you the minimum monthly sales figure you need and see how far you measure up in the early stages (with appropriate adjustments for seasonal factors).

You have already begun to see that profitability and business success is more complicated a question than just keeping in the black, or even the agreed red. You will now need to go further along this road and absorb the concept of the cash-flow forecast. This is not as difficult as it sounds, and there is certainly no need to panic, but it *is* important. It is often said that many small businesses are forced to go under despite having full order books and no problems in servicing their clients or customers; what has happened? Quite simply, the businesses have large bills to pay, unsympathetic creditors, and no money in the bank. The root problem may be that they are owed large sums, and cannot secure payment in time to meet their debts; or the problem may be a wider one – perhaps they needed to spend a great deal of money on equipment, or advertising, none of which was wasted, but which left them with insufficient funds to operate from day to day. In other words, they were short of capital. Whatever the reason, a cash-flow crisis has forced them out of business.

The job of the cash-flow forecast is to predict the level of the business bank account from month to month, and to ensure that there are always sufficient funds to operate; it can do this either by spreading expenditure over a period of several months (where this is possible), and/or by ensuring that sufficient advance capital has been borrowed to meet the inevitably heavier expenditure which will be encountered in the early months of trading.

In some respects the cash-flow forecast will resemble the monthly profit and loss accounts you have already been drawing up. But there are a number of key differences:

PROJECTED CASH-FLOW FORECAST (£s)

Month	1	2	3	4	5	6	7	8	9	10	11	12
INCOME												
Sales (include VAT)		5000	7000	7000	7000	7000	7000	7000	7000	7000	7000	7000
Loan	5000											
Investment	5000											
	10000	5000	7000	7000	7000	7000	7000	7000	7000	7000	7000	7000
EXPENDITURE												
Advertising	1500	1500	700	700	700	700	700	700	700	700	700	700
Research			2500	2500	2500	2500	2500	2500	2500	2500	2500	2500
Salaries (Drawings)	1667	1667	1667	1667	1667	1667	1667	1667	1667	1667	1667	1667
Bk-keeping			200	200	200	200	200	200	200	200	200	200
Rent			750			750			750			750
Motor	167	167	167	167	167	167	167	167	167	167	167	167
Travel	83	83	83	83	83	83	83	83	83	83	83	83
Postage	375	375	375	375	375	375	375	375	375	375	375	375
Stationery	1500						1500					
Audit												500
Bank charges						250						250
Maintenance		500										
Sundries			50	50	50	50	50	50	50	50	50	50
Interest			250			250			250			250
Computers		2000										
TOTALS	5292	6292	6742	5742	5742	6992	7242	5742	6742	5742	5742	7492
Surplus (Deficit)	4708	(1292)	258	1258	1258	8	(242)	1258	258	1258	1258	(492)
Balance c/f	4708	3466	3724	4982	6240	6248	5998	7256	7514	8772	10030	9538

1. In the profit and loss account you start with a zero balance; you are interested only in transactions within the month concerned. In the cash-flow forecast, you start with a balance of whatever capital you have invested or borrowed; you monitor that balance from month to month, carrying forward the closing balance from the earlier period at each stage.

2. In the profit and loss account you are not concerned with major capital expenditure, but only with the day-to-day running costs of the business; in the cash-flow forecast all expenditure must be included, since all expenditure affects the amount of cash available to your business.

3. In the profit and loss account you are concerned with the profit your business makes before you draw any money out of it for your own use; again, in the cash-flow forecast your personal drawings must be included, since they affect the cash balance of the business.

If you look at the example opposite, taken from the same business as the profit and loss account, you will see how these factors operate. The forecast is divided into two broad sections, receipts and expenditure; receipts will include money you invest or borrow at any stage, income from the work you do or products you sell (sales), and any additional income the business receives from, for example, the Enterprise Allowance Scheme. The figures you include for sales must, of course, be identical to those you drew up for your profit and loss account; however, if you did draw up three different accounts to demonstrate different levels of trading, it will not be necessary to draw up three cash-flow forecasts. Base the forecast on the second of the three trading levels, the one which represents the most realistic target for your first year of trading.

You may want to assume that no sales will be made for the first month, while you are principally engaged in making contacts and publicizing the products or services you offer; alternatively you may have a number of orders in the pipeline, or want to assume a more gradual increase in sales to the target figure. You may even decide after thinking about this more carefully that you will have to alter your profit and loss account again. Do so. It is very important that you arrive at figures which are shown to be realistic and which you are happy to subscribe to, no matter how many times you have to rewrite the draft. So adjust and readjust; move back and forth from profit and loss account to cash-flow forecast; make sure your figures are sustainable and that they add up.

In the example you will see that personal drawings have been included in the expenditure column; make sure you include a reasonable (though not excessive) figure. If you wish, quarterly VAT payments may be included in the cash-flow forecast, but not in the profit and loss account. The whole question of VAT registration is considered in Chapter 4, 'All about Money', and you may wish to read the relevant section now. But since any business with an annual turnover of more than about £20,000 is going to have to register, it will almost certainly concern you unless you are zero-rated or have virtually no expenses at all beyond your own drawings.

You will also see that the purchase of an inexpensive computer/word processor has been budgeted for in month two; this is to spread the early costs a little, bearing in mind the large advertising expense of the first month. At the bottom is a monthly surplus/deficit sum: quite simply the figure you arrive at when you subtract total expenditure from total income. This is helpful in showing which months are going to be especially heavy on expenditure and where you may be better to spread your costs a little. But even more important is your closing balance, which is arrived at by adding or subtracting the monthly surplus or deficit from the starting balance (carried forward from the previous month). If the business is a new one, you will start with a balance of nil, so it is important that the receipts in the first month are going to be enough to cope with early expenditure, when sales may not have reached their targets. You now begin to see why you need to borrow money to survive at the outset.

If you have an overdraft facility with a bank – the simplest form of borrowing and one which is likely to be enough if you are borrowing no more than £5000 – you may in addition want to include the actual bank balance at the bottom of the forecast. In the example, the owners of the business have each invested £2500 and they have agreed a loan of £5000 with a clearing bank. If this were an overdraft, the bank balance would be £5000 *not* £10,000, despite the fact that £10,000 had effectively been invested in the business. Keeping a record of the actual bank balance may help to establish when interest charges will be payable, so that these can be minimized by spreading certain costs.

And that is really all there is to it. The closing balance in any month represents the funds available at that point; as such it is important that it is never allowed to go below a certain level. What is that level? Clearly this will vary from business to business, and will depend on the kind of bill you might be faced with. If you are forced to spend hundreds of pounds for materials in advance of each job (perhaps you are an electrician or a builder), then you could run into problems unless your customers pay you promptly. In fact, you would be well advised to ask for a proportion of the cost in advance, so that at least you can cover the cost of your materials and continue trading.

Life is rarely as straightforward; you may find that when you are striving to establish yourself by offering more attractive terms than the local competition, there will be a temptation to accept any jobs offered, and not to worry too much about cash flow. This could be a mistake. You must learn to use the forecast, adjust it from month to month to take into account actual business experience, look ahead and see where problems could arise. If you have £5000 available, you would be insane to spend the bulk of it on computer equipment. But it might not be so obvious if you had not drawn up the forecast for the whole of the coming year so that you could see exactly where major expenditure would be necessary.

Presenting the business plan

You have your projected profit and loss account and your cash-flow forecast; you know what kind of business you want to run and you have the skills and experience required; you have done your market research and you know how much money you are looking to borrow. How do you put that information together and bowl over your crusty old bank manager with a really professional business plan?

The key is to keep it simple and businesslike; you are not writing a novel, or an autobiography. Set out the information under clear headings, starting on a clean sheet of paper for each section. Use good quality A4 paper, type your business plan or get somebody to type it for you, and type it double-spaced for easier reading. Have a separate cover sheet, with your own name, your trading name, address and telephone number. Put it all in a ring binder, or a clip-on slide binder (providing you can line up the pages neatly). Number the pages consecutively. Put the financial projections on their own at the back, referring to them in the text. None of these are essential prerequisites for a favourable hearing, but they will help to make the plan more readable and attractive. Have several copies made, and take a second one with you to your meeting with the bank manager.

If you are not clear about your figures, show the plan to a professional accountant and ask him or her to alter it if necessary – it will not cost you a fortune, and it may make all the difference if you are a little lacking in confidence. But even if you do get an accountant to draw up the final projections for you, you would still be well advised to go through the process of working out the figures for yourself first. It is the only way you can really get to know your business and any hidden costs; besides, you are going to have to answer questions about the plan, and your responses will be much more confident if you understand the figures and the reasoning behind them because you did the initial drafts yourself on your trusty pocket calculator.

A full business plan, adapted from the same research business you have already met, is available at the back of this book for reference (pp. 187–190); it may get you started. But please do express yourself in your own words as far as possible; in the end this will be far more convincing than any high-flown phrases.

If you have a go but still fail miserably to get down what you want to say on paper, refer to the main High Street banks. They all produce their own free business-plan packs. If you want to use these, all you have to do is fill in the answers to specific questions; it is unclear whether these standard business plans are intended for the benefit of the entrepreneur or the harassed bank manager with less than enough time on his hands. It is all a bit like filling in an application for a job, and you may feel it puts you in a defensive frame of mind, the wrong frame of mind. Much better that you express yourself positively, in your own terms; remember that the business plan is as much for your benefit as the bank's. But having said all that, there is no harm in your getting hold of these packs from the banks (just ask at your local branch) to see what kind of questions they are likely to ask you when you meet. And, of course, to make certain that there are no key areas you have left out of your own masterpiece.

Your first section should be about you. There is no need to include a full curriculum vitae; what the bank will need is some idea of your age, education and work experience; these should of course be tailored to emphasize those areas which impinge on the kind of business you propose to run. If you intend to build extensions, give full details of your apprenticeship and experience as a bricklayer, not your CSE in history.

Besides this, you may need to give an indication of your own personal assets – house, car and so on – together with any other income you enjoy. If you feel it is relevant, mention that your spouse has a steady job in local government and is only too pleased to support you in your decision to go it alone. But be careful to make sure that a spouse's income is not used as a substitute for drawing a living wage from your own business; it is not a successful business if it does not support you.

If this is your first business venture, you may want to compose a few lines on why you want to work for yourself and any relevant factors leading up to the decision you have made, coupled with reasons why you feel you would be a success in the business you have chosen. Do not overdo it; in many ways a person's character will be revealed more effectively in the business plan itself than in the platitudes about self-fulfilment and creativity he or she may write. And the bank manager will want to meet you, so he or she will also have an opportunity of gaining an impression of your personal style and image, and will be able to ask you questions about your background. Think of that meeting with your bank manager as your first business meeting, and deal with the bank as you would with a key client or supplier, always respectful but never grovelling.

And what about other personnel involved in the venture? If the business is not going to be a one-man band, it will be useful to include biographical data on anybody else, whether they be partners, or just part-timers. If you are forming a limited company, you will of course need to provide details of the shareholders and their relationship to each other, together with names of directors and perhaps their personal bankers. If you are a sole trader, you are your own business and things are much simpler, but that does not mean that there are no problems. Supposing that you are taken ill for a period of weeks? Is there anybody who could run the business competently in your absence, or at least ensure that existing customers were kept happy until you were able to return? The bank manager will be looking for signs that you have considered these types of problems and thought them through; it is not enough to hope that everything will run smoothly.

Now that you have introduced yourself, and any others involved in the venture with you, you need to introduce your business and come clean about how much you want to borrow and what you need the money for. Explain briefly what products or services you intend to offer, when you intend to begin trading and where from, whether you have any other sources of funding (e.g. that £2000 legacy from Great-aunt Agatha which has just fortuitously dropped into your lap). The bank manager will certainly be more impressed if you are putting some of your own money into the business, even if hundreds rather than thousands of pounds are involved. Explain that money needs to be borrowed to finance the start-up costs, and point to your cash-flow forecast to illustrate this, highlighting if necessary any major purchases which may need to be explained in more detail.

Show that you have obtained any licences you need to start trading, that you are aware of any legal restrictions, that you have planning permission (if appropriate) for what you intend to do. If you need to buy in raw materials or other supplies, show that you have costed these, and have other suppliers available should the need arise. How important will forces outside your control, such as the weather, be to your success? What happens if you need to expand and take on more staff? Will you be able to train the new personnel?

At this stage you may have convinced your bank manager that you understand the basics of business management. But unless your business idea can be shown to be a profitable one, forget it. The section of the business plan outlining your market needs to be well researched and provide real evidence for your claims. Hunches are not enough. If you claim that demand for your product or service is increasing, will increase and is unlikely to diminish in the foreseeable future, can you produce statistical evidence of this in government or trade publications? If not, have you conducted your own surveys to assess this? Have you really investigated your competition, posed as a potential customer to find out exactly what they are offering and for how much? What are your advantages as far as potential customers are concerned – location, quality, price? Have you drawn up a realistic budget for the first year's marketing, and included it in your projected profit and loss account? You have to be able to answer each of these questions if you are to demonstrate to your bank that you are a safe bet.

There is no need to spend much time commenting on the projected accounts themselves – set out the figures in neat columns, use plain English for your subject headings, and make sure these are self-explanatory. It is worth concluding the text of your plan with a short section setting out precisely how much you want to borrow, the type of finance you require, and when it will be needed. In general, think in terms of an overdraft if you simply need working capital to enable the business to survive over the first months. If what you are looking for is intended to finance a specific purchase, such as a vehicle, then what bankers call a term loan will be more appropriate, with a precise timetable for capital and interest repayments worked out in advance.

You should consider very carefully whether the amount you are looking to borrow really is sufficient for your working capital needs; is there a margin to cope with unforeseen circumstances? It is better to ask for a slightly larger overdraft than you really need, and to avoid the embarrassment of having to come back two months later to explain that your initial figures were incorrect. After all, the whole point of an overdraft is its flexibility; you are only borrowing as much as you really need at any one time.

What you do need to demonstrate in the event of a term loan is the relationship between your own projected profitability and cash flow and the anticipated repayments. What turnover figure will be needed to break even, and how quickly will your business begin to generate excess cash? It is common for capital repayments to be deferred for a period of, say, a year, to enable the business to establish itself in the early stages; will this be necessary in your case? Have you considered the effects of variations in the interest-rate level, and how your projections might need to be adjusted as a result? And what happens when things go wrong; have you devised contingency plans to act on if problems arise?

This may seem a negative conclusion, but the banker's primary aim is to protect the investment of the bank. You, too, need to consider the maximum losses the business might sustain, and how you would make up that shortfall so as not to court bankruptcy. The bank may ask you to secure the loan personally, on any assets you possess; if the loan is secured against the value of an insurance policy, for example, the bank will probably require you to deposit the policy documents with them until the loan has been repaid. You may not have to provide security for the whole of a loan, but in general a bank is unlikely to lend unsecured any more than the owner of the business is prepared to invest personally.

Again, the question of insurance will have to be covered in your business plan – not only must your premises and assets be covered against theft and fire, it will also be essential, if you are a sole trader, for life insurance to be taken out to ensure that any creditors (including the bank) can be repaid in the event of your sudden death. Do not attempt to sweep such matters under the carpet; the bank manager knows you would much prefer to spend all your time talking about the wonderful ideas you have to bring in more business, or about how unique and exciting the business idea itself is. Fair enough. But he would be less than fair, to you as well as to the bank, if he did not take a cautious view as well. Ask yourself how you would feel if you were sitting on the other side of the desk, preparing to lend several thousand pounds to an almost complete stranger.

So be businesslike. Send your plan to the bank manager well in advance of your need for cash, with a covering letter requesting a meeting. Follow up with a telephone call, to confirm that the plan has indeed arrived and to make an appointment. Dress smartly for the meeting, talk confidently about your business and your hopes, answer each of the questions put to you. If your plan covers all the points outlined, if it is clearly presented, if you have identified both your market and your financial needs, you should get what you are looking for. At last your business will be off the ground.

The High Street banks are often criticized for their unwillingness to take risks on lending money to new businesses, but at a level of £5000 or less you are unlikely to find this a great problem. There are, of course, plenty of other sources of capital, and the Small Firms Centre will be happy to discuss them with you, but if the first bank manager does turn you down, your best bet will be to try another one. And not necessarily even another bank; strange as it may seem, individual branch managers are human beings, with their own prejudices and experiences, and you may receive the green light from the manager of another branch just a couple of miles away, simply because he or she knows a bit more about your field of interest and the potential it has. However, if you have been turned down by a succession of lenders, consider what is wrong with your business plan, and seek help from one or more of the bodies named in the first chapter. It may be that a few adjustments to your costings could make all the difference. On the other hand (and this is perhaps the most common problem), your marketing plan may be thin and unconvincing; you have not worked out the potential of your ideas, who your customers are, or what they need.

3

BRINGING IN BUSINESS

Principles of marketing

What on earth does anybody mean by marketing? Is it just a fancy name for selling, as most people think? No; the first thing you need to understand is that while selling is concerned with distributing your services or products to your customers or clients, marketing is a much wider concept. In marketing you consider your very reason for existence, what kind of business you are, who your customers are, who your competitors are. You must, after all, decide what you are going to sell and who you are going to sell it to before you can begin selling.

Obviously, you have already considered some of these questions at the outset, in the days when you were only beginning to think about starting your own business and when you were drawing up that first business plan. All the different ingredients which help to make up a successful business venture impinge on each other, and cannot be arbitrarily divided between chapters; you will need to bear them all in mind all the time. But if you do now have your finance organized, it is no bad moment to go back to basics before you actually start trading and take another, more detailed look at your marketing plan.

What kind of business are you? You might think that a stupid question – obviously you are a window-cleaner, or an electrician, or you make and sell jewellery. Well, perhaps. But look at it from the customer's point of view; try to decide what those customers need, what else they might be persuaded to buy from you. If you are going from door to door offering your window-cleaning services, you are in a good position to spot the mountains of rubbish piling up on the patio at the back of the house; perhaps the owners do not have the transport available for a trip or trips to the nearest municipal dump, perhaps they are simply too lazy to hire a skip. Either way, they might well be prepared to pay you £10 or so to get rid of it for them. In the same way, you can persuade them that their front or back garden could be tidied up and made to look really nice for a few pounds. People who have just moved in will have more than enough to do decorating and sorting out their furniture to want to get stuck in to the garden and will probably be glad of the offer. From your point of view, by gaining extra business from one customer you have saved yourself the effort of having to persuade somebody else to have their windows cleaned; the more work you do for one customer, and the better you do it, the more likely it is that your customer will think of you again when he or she has another job and has no idea whom to ask. A simple example perhaps, but a sound business principle none the less.

If you make and sell your own jewellery at craft fairs and markets, your customers will see you as a market trader rather than a craft worker. So why not try selling other people's products as well, on a commission basis? By broadening your product base, you will attract more people to the stall and have a better chance of selling your own jewellery as well.

The key point to note is: do not fall into the trap of defining your business merely by the service or product you first thought of; define it in terms of your market. If you examine a market first and foremost, other products and services will come to mind and may be easily combined with your initial idea to give you the edge over your competitors. But how do you draw up a profile of the market you are aiming at? If you are starting a business from scratch, how do you know what or where your market is?

For many people starting one of the kinds of businesses outlined in this book, the market will be a local one, defined geographically. This is certainly going to be the case if you are providing most types of personal service. But do not make the mistake of assuming that, because you know your area and your neighbours, you know your market well enough not to have to think about it. In the case of the window-cleaner based on a large estate, the kind of customer might not vary much from one house to the next; perhaps it is essentially a modern estate of young couples, many with children, who tend to move within the estate to a larger house when the need arises. Such a geographical community of relatively prosperous home-owners would indeed provide a solid base for a personal service like window-cleaning, gardening, painting and decorating.

But most localities are not, of course, as homogeneous as this. People know the streets in their own town, village or neighbourhood; they know where to find the sheltered housing schemes and the nursing homes, the run-down council blocks and the detached mansions with their pillars and covered swimming-pools, the rows of near-identical Edwardian terraces and the rows of near-identical mock-Tudor semis. You will know your market, too, if it is geographically based; use that knowledge. If, for example, you intend a leaflet drop of 5000, target your leaflets to the best areas for your kind of product or service. There is not a lot of point in offering building work or electrical services in an area where the bulk of the property is rented; on the other hand, a desirable estate of ex-council properties, most of which have now been bought by sitting tenants keen to proclaim that fact to their neighbours, might be among the most fertile of districts.

So what you need to do right at the start, preferably as part of the business plan, is to define your market in terms of the income, status and location of your potential customers, and not just in terms of the uniqueness of your product or service. Where necessary you may also have to bring into play other characteristics such as sex or educational background. Remember that one of the keys to a successful marketing plan is accurate research. Do not allow yourself to get away with the attitude that there will not be any available data on the market you are looking at; there is data available on anything if you know where to look. To take the simplest example once again, your reference library will provide information on the local population by age, home ownership, social class, ethnic background and a host of other factors, broken down into local government wards of a few thousand people and taken mainly from the ten-yearly national census. Much of this could be out of date, but it will provide a basis of hard fact which can be added to in the light of your own experience. Similarly, Chambers of Commerce will help with data on local market trends and may be able to give you ideas on what types of product or service are growing in importance in your area, or equally what seems to be lacking or doing badly.

Of course, your product or service may indeed be of a highly specialized nature, and require specialized advertising through trade or hobby journals with national or even international circulation. But even here – perhaps especially here – you are going to have to make firm predictions about the kind of potential customer you are aiming for. And that has big implications, not just for the kind of advertising or other selling technique you intend to utilize, but for the identification of your competitors and how you are going to stay ahead of them. Again, research will be invaluable; this time you may find it helpful to contact societies or trade associations for those with interests in a particular subject; send a SAE and they may give you information about themselves, their facilities and their membership, so you can judge how fast this is expanding, whether there is any geographical concentration, what journals the members read.

You may be in a situation like our hypothetical window-cleaner who learns that nobody has ever been round to clean the windows on that equally hypothetical new estate, and has spotted what he sees as an entirely new market, with no competitors to mess things up. Or equally, you may be like the small ancestry research firm whose business plan was analysed and whose service seemed so esoteric that it was a simple matter to identify *all* other British businesses in the same field, obtain copies of their sales literature and details of their marketing techniques and personnel. But if your business is a more mainstream one, like electrical or building work, you should certainly contact trade associations, who will provide lists of members and details of how to go about joining, which could be invaluable as a marketing tool itself.

This kind of research is fairly passive, but there are other things you can do too. As we have seen, you can scour local newspapers or specialist journals, the Yellow Pages and town directories. Make lists of any businesses who seem to be even remotely offering a similar service or product to your own. Write off to them (you can use a friend's name and address if you are shy about this) pretending to be a potential customer and requesting copies of their sales literature. Gauge the response time, the first impressions of the material. Did they follow up with another letter or a phone call? How close is their business to yours in terms of market as well as product/service? If you are brave, you can ring them up, ask them questions about what they do, try to discover how busy they are, how they cost their service or product. You could even get them to give you names of satisfied customers so that you could inspect the work, still in the guise of the potential customer, of course. Why are you doing all this? Because if you are going to compete against other businesses yours must have something unique which makes your potential customers buy from you rather than anybody else. Marketing people call this the 'unique selling proposition', but there is no need for you to employ such jargon unless you want to.

Most people, when faced with the need to differentiate themselves from their competitors, think that all they need to do to bring in the business is reduce the price of the product or service. If they are the cheapest, they think, everybody must go for them. Not so. Price is rarely the most important factor in the kind of business you are likely to be concerned with. Price wars have their value when you have millions of pounds to spend, or lose, in driving your competitors away; they may also have their uses if you are selling expensive consumer durables by well-known names, and the customer has little to do other than visit a succession of showrooms on a Saturday afternoon, check the stock, and inspect the credit agreements. But you only have to think about your own experiences of using small or local businesses to see that the 'price is everything' argument is nonsense. Most people will have asked for valuations from a number of estate agents, or quotations from removal firms, or electricians or painters and decorators. If you think hard about those occasions, and think what caused you to make your final choice, you will have a real insight into the 'unique selling proposition' you are striving to find. Perhaps one of the estate agents was more pleasant, less aggressive in his approach, and seemed to have a genuine interest in your house and what you had done to it. Or perhaps that second electrician who was charging a bit more went into much more detail about the work he had to do, about replacing the fuse-box or re-routing the telephone wire, and perhaps you just felt that much more confident about asking him to rewire your house.

Of course there is a relationship between cost and quality and it would be stupid to pretend otherwise. The estate agent who was more pleasant and less aggressive and admired the pictures in your living-room may not be offering you anything of substance at the end of the day; many agents would argue that décor contributes almost nothing towards the value of a house and little towards its saleability, and it may not be enough to be nice. Perhaps a harder head would look at how high a profile the agent has in the neighbourhood, and his or her subsequent capacity to attract the maximum number of potential buyers, as well as the commission charged.

A balanced approach to this whole question is to see price as a factor, and a significant factor, but only one factor among many. You may feel that the old saying about the customer choosing the middle one of three estimates has much to commend it; the other side to this is that there is no way in which you can possibly market your service on this basis. Every firm in your line will have its own method of calculating an estimate, so you cannot possibly know what other estimates any potential customer has had (unless you ask directly, and if you do that you are rather giving the game away). So we come back once more to the whole question of a 'unique selling proposition' and what you have to offer your market beyond just a good price.

We have already touched on the possibility of selling other services or products to the same customers, and you must certainly always keep a lookout for any such opportunities. But use existing customers to develop in other ways too. If you are offering any kind of research or consultancy service, you will probably find that prompt attention and a smart presentation of the client's report are the kinds of things the clients will willingly pay more for, in so far as anybody ever willingly pays more for anything. Since a greater efficiency in your turnaround of work and a more imaginative approach to the design of your product are not necessarily things that are going to cost you, you can in this way increase the profit margin on each sale without a great deal of difficulty. And you will have customers or clients who are even more pleased with you and willing to recommend you to their friends. It may surprise you to think of such matters under the marketing umbrella, but then that is another lesson you must learn when you are in business for yourself; everything relevant to your business affects everything within that business. So do not make the mistake of thinking about things in isolation.

In the end, marketing is all about knowing who your customers are and who they might be, what they want and what you can provide them with. It involves making sure you are aware of all the possible corporate or individual outlets for your products – if you are used to dealing with other small private businesses it may not have occurred to you to try voluntary or public sector organizations and assess their needs – but also making sure that you are providing something special, something they cannot get elsewhere at the same or any other price. It involves the recognition that you are in business to identify the needs of others and to fill those needs.

How much do I charge?

Even after reading the previous section, you may not feel that pricing has a lot to do with marketing; perhaps you work on the principle that there is a 'rate for the job' you are offering your potential customers, that all your competitors are charging about the same, that you intend to undercut them just enough to pull in the orders for the first few months. Or perhaps you have simply priced your products or services on the basis of the costings you did for the business plan, adding on a percentage to cover overheads and another percentage for profit. If you did do that, you would certainly not be alone, but you would equally certainly not have understood the principles of marketing. It all underlines the value of reading this chapter before you put together the business plan.

Obviously, those costings are vital and you do have to work them out before you can decide how much you should charge. But they only tell you your minimum price per unit of production, the price you cannot go below because if you do you are not even covering the intrinsic costs of labour and materials.

Nor can you even safely base your charges on those of your competitors. How do you know that the competitors are even making a profit? Or if they are, that their costs are not dramatically lower than yours, thus making it impossible for you to sustain a business on the same lines? Again, what your competitors charge is important information, part of the market research you must do when you are thinking through your ideas at the outset, but such information cannot be used as the basis of a marketing plan. If it is, you are looking at your market the wrong way round. What you need to decide is what you are selling and why it is unique, and what your customers will pay for it.

This concept, that the value of any product or service is simply what the market will pay, is easy to understand in an abstract and extreme example, like the different value of the same loaf of bread in a famine or in a feast; it is much less easy to cope with when you are faced with the day-to-day problem of what to charge your own customers in the real world. But it is worth making the point that if customers are paying so much for the inferior service offered by your competitor, it follows that they will pay more for the superior service offered by you. Similarly, if you enter the market offering what you claim is a better service at a lower price, will they believe you? You are just as likely, probably more likely, to attract the business by charging a little more, provided of course that you get across the point that your service really is better and in what way it is better. And by charging a little more, instead of cutting your profit margins to the bone, you will be better able to withstand temporary fluctuations in interest rates or in the cost of materials.

If you are offering relatively expensive consultancy services, for example, it may be appropriate to quote an hourly rate for your work rather than an all-inclusive fee. But the same principle should still apply. Calculate your costs per hour first, but price your service on the basis of what it is worth to your clients, and on the basis that what they are buying from you is something they cannot get elsewhere, or at least not so conveniently. Never sell yourself short.

Look at the mobile hairdressing example again. For people in that kind of business, there is a temptation to argue that they should charge less than a town-centre hairdresser, because they do not have the expensive premises to keep up. What they should be emphasizing is the unique personal service they are offering their clients, the money and time they are saving people who would otherwise have to make a special journey into town. Given that they will have worked for one of the town-centre establishments before setting up on their own, they should not lack confidence in their ability to provide a service of at least the same quality, and charge accordingly.

This is easier said than done, and if you are involved in your first business venture it is easy to be overawed by your competitors and what you see as their established reputation. You must try to forget the history of those other businesses and take a hard look at them now. You are confident that they are not supplying adequately the needs of your target market; you are confident that you can supply that market. Why are you not confident enough to charge your customers what they will see as a reasonable price for the unique service or products you are offering them? If you have done your market research thoroughly, if you can supply what your customers need, pricing should not be a barrier to success.

Your marketing plan

Given that you have identified your target market, and priced your service or product based on its value to that market, it is fair to say that you are likely to experience some resistance from potential customers until you have proved yourself to be reliable. To help get beyond that initial resistance, to help fill up your order book with customers you will satisfy and who will then generate more customers, you need a plan of action. That plan will be made up of two broad components:

- The analysis of your market and your competitors
- The location, organization and promotion of your business

The first of these components has been broadly covered in the earlier part of this chapter and in the chapter concerned with your business plan. It is this part which has told you that you really do have a business – not just a hunch with no evidence to back it up – and which has enabled you to persuade your bank manager to lend you money to get that business started. Now that you are up and running you need to look in more detail at the second of the two components: how you reach your customers, how you persuade them to buy from you, how you keep them happy and willing to buy again. In the first instance, you are probably going to have to think about advertising.

Advertising is just another of the words would-be business people come up against and find scary. If you are told that you should be quite capable of doing your own advertising, you might even panic. But think for a moment: with your initial £5000 capital, you are not talking about big-budget TV commercials; doing your own advertising need only mean an ability to write sales letters, simple brochures, leaflets and magazine advertisements. Of course, if you really are totally unable to express yourself on paper, and find the very thought terrifying, you can always go to an advertising consultant (check the names in *The Creative Handbook* at your library, and get quotes and samples from at least three freelance consultants). But there are many advantages in learning how to do it yourself: only you really know everything there is to know about the product or service you are offering; only you have done the research on your market and your competitors, and know precisely why the customer needs your service or product. Why not take that extra step and put the knowledge you have gained into effect to work for you?

Of course there are always cautionary words to digest before spending any money in business, and advertising is no exception:

- Do not spend money on advertising unless you are certain that your product or service is a good one
- Do not spend money on advertising unless you are certain that you can cope with a subsequent increase in demand for what you are offering
- Do not spend money on advertising unless you are certain that your product or service is different from and better than those of your competitors
- Do not spend money on advertising unless you have a clear idea of the person you are offering your product or service to

You will already be complaining that you have been through most if not all of these points when you were drawing up the business plan and doing the initial market research. Good. Think about them again. They are so vital to the success of your business that they must constantly be in your mind.

What sort of advertising budget should you think in terms of when you draw up your initial marketing plan? You will remember the figure of 10 per cent of turnover which was mentioned when you were putting together the business plan. Most people with marketing experience, and perhaps your bank manager, will see such a figure as excessive, though all will agree that different percentages apply for different businesses, and even that it may be wrong to express an advertising budget in terms of percentage turnover. The 10 per cent figure was included partly because you have to have a costing to put in your business plan, and partly to illustrate the fact that in your initial year you may have to spend a lot more than you would like to get your name and your product or service established. Do not stick too rigidly to that budget when you actually start trading, then.

A far better approach is to decide which options are available to you and which of these will promote your business most effectively; in other words, work out what you want to do first and then tot up the cost. If the cost does go above the budgeted figure, you will find it easier to make economies if you have worked out your priorities in advance.

Journal advertising

With a £5000 capital limit, the only mass media you need concern yourself with initially are newspapers and magazines. As you establish your market position locally, you may be interested in reaching a wider audience through local radio, or posters on buses or station platforms. But leave these for later. What you should certainly do, however, is exploit the opportunities in the Yellow Pages and the Thomson local directory for your area. You get a line entry free of charge, but every small business should take out a display space as well, perhaps with a line illustration of, say, a removal van if you are in the removals business. Remember that anybody looking in such a publication already has, by definition, a need to satisfy, and will buy from one of the firms which attracts his or her attention.

Which newspapers? If you are locally based you would obviously be well advised to check out your local newspapers, both paid for and free; even if you are offering an unusual service to a national or international audience, national newspapers with their huge and disparate circulations and correspondingly high rates for advertising space, are unlikely to be cost-effective. When you are buying space in the press, always retain in your mind an image of the person you are targeting; ask yourself which newspaper or magazine will enable you to reach the maximum number of people of that type. In general terms, local papers of whatever sort are most likely to work if you are appealing to the average man or woman; if you are selling to a more specialized market you will want to look more closely at trade or professional journals.

Paid newspaper or freesheet? The advantage of a freesheet is that it does reach everybody; even the most widely read traditional newspaper will not be bought by more than one in two households in its catchment area. The disadvantage is of course that the quality of editorial will almost certainly be lower in the free publication, meaning that many people will throw it away on sight, and even those who read it may give it (and its advertising) less credence than they would if they had paid for it. Local newspapers vary so much that you will have to use your own judgement to a large degree; call up the representatives and get them to come and chat to you; look carefully at the production and editorial quality, and at the advertisements they already carry (where do your competitors advertise?). Learn to make an informed decision after you have obtained all the facts; do not let yourself be browbeaten or persuaded to take out 'free' publicity in exchange for running an expensive advertisement.

Again, you will need to be in possession of all the facts before you make a decision on the size of the advert you want to place, but in the case of local publications you will be looking at display rather than classified space. If you are selling something of interest to a high proportion of the buying public (and if you are not you should probably consider other forms of advertising anyway) it is generally wise to buy as much space as you can afford in a few consecutive issues, rather than place a tiny and unnoticed advert every week for several months.

Another important question to consider is where you want the advert to appear. Many local newspapers have a separate section where local builders, electricians, decorators or removal firms advertise their services, and this could be a good bet if it is not already too crowded and you feel you can attract attention. But you may prefer to buy space in the sports section, for example, or the women's page, if you feel that your product or service is aimed at those interest groups within the local community. If you are in the mail-order field, and want to attach a coupon for customers to send back, make sure you place your advert in the bottom left corner of a left-hand page, or the bottom right corner of a right-hand page; that way readers can get at the coupon without destroying the newspaper.

You will probably be aware of most of the local publications circulating in your immediate vicinity, though it is always worth asking the freesheets in particular whether they produce a glossy magazine for distribution to the more salubrious households and streets, at least if you are offering an upmarket product or service. But when it comes to the trade and technical journals which exist for almost every professional or indeed amateur interest under the sun, and which you will certainly want to tap if you are involved in a more specialized operation, you will need a reference source. *British Rate and Data* (BRAD) is useful because it provides you in most cases with audited circulation figures as well as the cost of advertising space, and it also has the merit of being updated monthly. It is, however, prohibitively expensive to buy, so ask for it at a good reference library.

It is more important to study specialist journals carefully in advance, to gauge the style of advertising, to assess the kind of reader, to pick up on big news stories within the magazine's field of interest which might tie in with what you have to offer. Write to any such journal and they will be delighted to send you their 'media pack', usually comprising a sample copy of the magazine, rate cards with details of copy deadlines, and often a readership survey, which is especially useful in telling you whether the person who reads the magazine is the person you are aiming at.

How do you actually write your copy? Once again, the need for preparation should be emphasized. You must know how your competitors advertise their products or services, and how you differ from them. You must know all about your own products and services, and what makes them unique. You should have an image in your mind of the man or woman you are trying to reach, so that you can imagine yourself talking to that one person when you write. By imagining yourself talking to one person, you ensure that you have indeed pinpointed your market sufficiently for an advertising campaign to work, and at the same time you help yourself to put your message into everyday colloquial prose, which is vitally important.

It is impossible in the space available here to take you through the process of writing a good advert in any detail. But there are some principles you would do well to take note of:

- Write when you are enthusiastic about your business and what you are offering
- Pick on one persuasive reason for people to buy from you; make it into a headline. Are you offering something new or exclusive, are you offering anything free, is anything you do quicker or cheaper than your competitors?
- Use simple, everyday words and phrases
- Make sure the reader knows what to do next – 'Ring now', 'Write today', 'Order on the form below'

If you are seriously interested in the whole concept of doing your own advertising, you may want to buy or borrow *Do Your Own Advertising* by Alastair Crompton (Hutchinson Better Business Guides). Other areas covered by Crompton include a step-by-step guide to writing an eight-page brochure, and when and how to use photographs; his book is very much geared towards those with low budgets, and is thoroughly recommended.

One thing you must do whenever you place advertising with a journal or newspaper is keep a track of the volume and calibre of response. If you are working on a mail-order basis, this can be done fairly easily by including a different Department number with the address of each advertisement: Dept 1 for *The Loamshire Times*, Dept 2 for the *Widget-Makers Gazette* and so on. If you are expecting most of your inquiries to be by telephone, you will simply have to ask, unless the inquirer volunteers the information at the outset, as many will. It is also good practice to file away a cutting of each advertisement you place for future reference.

The calibre of the response means the volume of actual business you receive from the source in question, as opposed to the volume of inquiries which never lead to anything. If you are selling a fairly expensive luxury item or service, you may find that advertising in some magazines or newspapers brings you many letters from people who cannot afford to buy, while a corresponding advertisement in a journal with a similar but more affluent readership might bring in fewer letters but ultimately more money. If this happens, it means that your initial market research has not accurately pinpointed the section of the public who may buy your products.

There are two morals here: pinpoint your market as accurately as possible before you start spending money; and when you do find that certain of your chosen media produce a far better response (as you almost certainly will), be prepared to switch resources to take into account this new information. You should be constantly in touch with your market, both through your own existing customers and through your reference sources, constantly searching for new outlets through which you can promote your business; only that way can you stay ahead of the game.

Leaflet drops

These are excellent for the locally based new firm trying to establish itself, but you must be prepared to spend money on good-quality paper or card, to give that all-important first impression of a high-quality outfit. Take time putting your strong selling points across, go for a bold headline, use line drawings if you can to increase interest. Above all, make sure the recipient knows what to do next, when and whom to call or where to visit you. The great advantage of such handbills is that they can be delivered at precisely the time you want, for maximum impact, and of course you can target them by street or even house.

Direct mail

This works well if your target market is one with easily identifiable characteristics. Examples: age 30–40, sex male, geographical location north-east England, university graduate, director of a company with a turnover of £1–£2 million. The advantage is that people are much more likely to see and to respond to a personally addressed letter than to a conventional advertisement; you can of course do a test mailing of perhaps 1000 letters, and see where it gets you. The Post Office has representatives in each district who will be more than happy to explain their various special deals to you, which may involve, for example, a Business Reply service. If you are serious about direct mail as a major part of your marketing plan, you should certainly contact the Post Office first of all and perhaps also get hold of a copy of *The Post Office Direct Mail Handbook* as your bible.

The hard part is drawing up the lists. It is easy enough to put together your own if you are only interested in certain types of business, or in members of professional institutions; another profitable mailing list will be your own ex-customers, who should certainly be told about new products or services they might be interested in. Technical journals may be prepared to distribute your material to all or some of their subscribers. Beyond such obviously available names, you may need to rent mailing lists from one of the many companies in the field, but they do not come cheap, and before embarking on large expenditure of this nature you should think very carefully about whether this is really the best way to reach your target market.

A response of between one and two per cent is a good average for most direct mailshots; certainly a response of five per cent would be sensational. Bear this in mind when you calculate your costs in terms of postage, and always remember to cost your own time or the time of whoever types and stuffs the envelopes for you; if the costs are such that you cannot work happily within the average percentage response, forget it. It should be clear that direct mail is unlikely to appeal unless you are expecting your customers to spend substantial sums.

If you are sending a mailshot to people you have had no previous contact with, it is silly to waste time and money on a lavish brochure. What you want is a strong sales letter, attracting the attention of the potential customer so that he or she calls or writes with his or her specific needs. At that point you can afford to be more expansive.

Sales letters

You could be sending these either to people who have responded in writing to an advertisement, or as part of a 'cold' mailshot; the broad principles will remain the same, and follow a famous selling sequence:

- attract Attention
- arouse Interest
- create Desire
- incite Action

What does all this mean? Well, you can attract attention partly by presentation: smart envelope (try a different colour), good-quality paper, short, indented paragraphs, important points underlined in another colour. But more important is that first paragraph or page. Whatever you do, do not use one of the boring letter openings you will probably be familiar with: 'I am writing to you because' or 'Thank you for your inquiry of the 3rd inst'. You must sound as if you were writing the headline for an advertisement, with the biggest selling point, the biggest promise you can offer. If you like, you can even put the first sentence into capitals, like a headline. But it is vital that people read that first sentence. If they read that, they may go on to read the first paragraph, the first page, and then the second; if you cannot hook them at the outset, you have no chance.

You then take the reader through all the things you can do for him or her, perhaps using link phrases such as 'And that's only the first part' or 'And let's not forget'. Next you think of all the objections which the reader could possibly raise, and answer them with hard facts. Finally, and as always, you must make it absolutely clear what you want the reader to do, and that you want it done now. Reply-paid or Freepost cards are useful here, but they need to be reinforced with a phrase like: 'Post the card right away, so you won't forget.' Even better if you have the recipient's address already typed on to the card, so he or she only has to check it and pop it into the post-box. A golden rule with any form of advertising: the easier you make it for people to respond, the more they will respond.

Other forms of promotion

Anything that costs your business nothing is worth having, as long as it does not damage your business image; it follows that a concerted effort to procure free publicity in newspapers, magazines or local radio is bound to be worth while. Again, you could employ a public relations consultant, who will know which media might be interested in running a story about you, and will be experienced in putting together a well-crafted press release. But if you are capable of drafting good advertising copy and strong sales letters or handbills, you are capable of drafting a press release which will attract attention. You know your own business better than anybody, and if there is an interesting story there (and there almost always is) you are the person most likely to know about it.

What most people fail to realize is how much 'news' of this kind local newspapers will print; this is especially true of the freesheets, who employ few reporters or editorial staff and will often print a well-written press release in its entirety. All you need do is take a good-quality sheet of A4 paper, and head it Press Release. Make sure you provide your name and a telephone number where you can be contacted for further information. Put in plenty of lively quotes, from yourself or (better) from prominent local customers; enclose an attractive photograph, preferably showing your business in action. Remember that when you are starting up you are news by definition, especially if you are the only business of your type in the area, though clearly you will be better placed to write an interesting piece about yourself if you are researching the histories of businesses rather than rewiring their offices. That may seem bad luck if you are in a mainstream business like building or plumbing, but the fact is that people tend to be interested in the unusual.

You could try writing about some of the unusual things you have seen in your plumbing career (you might even call it 'Confessions of a Plumber'), but here you would probably be better getting a professional freelance to interview you and write up the article, or alternatively speaking to a journalist on the newspaper you are targeting. Press releases will also be of little interest to a trade or technical journal, and if you have done something startling in a specialized field, your best bet might be to pick up the telephone and speak to the editor, preparing yourself in advance to give him or her the salient points of your news story. If you can produce a photograph, so much the better; animals, children and cuddly old people are still as good a bet as ever they were.

Another cheap way of promoting your business more effectively is to take a long, hard look at your own image. For example, do you use a van to take you from job to job? If so, why not have your name, address, telephone number and logo painted on both sides in bold colours? It is surprising how many firms fail to promote themselves to their potential customers at even this basic level; if you do not even say who you are and what you do, how do you expect people to remember you when they next need somebody in your line of business? This takes you back to the question of choosing a good name for your outfit: J. Smith, Painter and Decorator might be fine if you are operating very locally as a one-man band, though even here a logo (perhaps a paintbrush or stepladders) might help you to stick in people's minds.

Make sure that logo appears on your letterhead, on your invoices, on your business cards. Have a good look at that letterhead and the other stationery; use more than one colour, not just boring black on white. When considering which typeface to use, consider the kind of image you want to present; many businesses look terribly old-fashioned with their Gothic script, and if you want to project yourself as classic, but still up to date, Times New Roman is more appealing. Get your printer to discuss the possibilities with you.

Ultimately you are your business in the eyes of your customers or clients; unless the work you are doing is manual, you ought to dress smartly – how formally will depend on what you do (a designer will not be expected to dress like a management consultant). If you are doing manual work in other people's houses or offices, make sure you leave things as clean and tidy as you can. People really notice, and it is all part of the customer relations which is a vital part of bringing in business.

Another good tip is to record a few of your telephone conversations. How pleasant and confident did you sound? Did you listen to what the customer was saying, did you let him or her finish without interruption? Remember that the telephone may be the first contact many customers have with you, and if you sound fed-up or disorganized or unable to answer legitimate questions about your work, they will probably look elsewhere. Try to make sure, incidentally, that you return telephone calls on the same day if at all possible, and that you do the same with postal inquiries; a prompt response does create a good image, and helps you to avoid backlogs which can easily be forgotten. You may find that in the early stages, when you cannot afford to pay for secretarial help, you have to spend an hour or two each evening getting your paperwork up to date. It is time well spent, whatever you may feel at the time after a heavy day.

By now you should have a clear plan to bring in business for your first year of trading. Never stop there. Remember to monitor the cost and effectiveness of your advertising, to keep track of your competitors and any improvements they make in response to you, to use your financial projections to identify problems such as increases in the cost of materials and what you should do about them. Never fall into the trap of simply increasing or decreasing your price in response to a problem; business is more complicated than that.

This book has said nothing about the opportunities for export, because it is a fundamental principle that you should never use overseas markets as an alternative when you fail to establish yourself in UK markets. Only when you are established here should you consider export, and that is unlikely to be in your first year; when you are ready, talk to the Small Firms Service, and the British Overseas Trade Board.

There is one problem associated with bringing in business which you may not have considered: the problem of bringing in too much business too quickly, of being inundated with work you cannot perform, and money for which you are unable to provide goods or services. There are two solutions: one is to proceed very cautiously at the beginning with any advertising or publicity you initiate, testing the water first with leaflet drops of a few hundred rather than a few thousand; the other is to make sure that your office systems and monetary controls are as efficient as you can make them, so that when fluctuations in income do arise, you are able to cope with the situation without having a nervous breakdown. It is to those systems and controls that you must now turn.

4

ALL ABOUT MONEY

Keeping it simple

You might look at the title of this chapter and groan. You might think it deals with book-keeping and tax returns and invoicing and . . . all the boring things about running a business you want to leave until your first cheques are coming in and you have a full order book. Well, it does deal with those things. But if you learn nothing else from this book you must learn that you cannot afford to see the question of money as a subsidiary issue. If you wait until the cheques are coming in you will be too busy with other jobs to get your accounting procedures sorted out; you must do it now.

You have seen how the business plan is about far more than just raising capital by impressing your bank manager with your financial projections; it incorporates you, your resources, your market, to give an overall view of where you think your business should be heading. You can use it to monitor your progress, adjusting your sales targets, for example, in the light of your actual marketing experience. But you can only use that business plan and its financial projections if you have accurate data with which to assess your progress. And that means proper attention to your book-keeping, to credit control, to sales and purchase invoices, to tax, to all the things you see as boring and inessential. They are tools to help you proclaim your successes and spot approaching problems; they are nothing to be afraid of and they *are* vital to your success.

The point that there is nothing to be afraid of is one worth making. A lot of people are apt to think that book-keeping requires special skills; although they would be quite capable of marketing their products or services, and building up a strong base of clients or customers, the accounting and 'business management' side of things would defeat them and lead to a horrendous financial mess from which it would be impossible to extricate themselves. Things have not been helped by the plethora of small-business books which have appeared in the last few years, which have often been written by accountants or bankers who go into great technical detail about raising new equity capital or calculating financial ratios, without bearing in mind the fact that such information is not essential to the average start-up situation and may put off large numbers of people who might otherwise be extremely interested in the idea of self-employment or running a small business.

So please remember this: anybody who is capable of ordering their own affairs without getting into too much trouble is capable of running the accounts side of their own small business. And what if you are *not* capable of ordering your own domestic affairs? You are always forgetting to pay off the minimum balance on your monthly credit-card statements, you routinely fail to note on your cheque stub the amount of the cheque and its purpose, you never know who owes you money or how much they owe you, you accumulate huge fines for the failure to return library books. Surely, that kind of person cannot run their own business effectively. Well, maybe, maybe not. If you really are good at the marketing, quality control, customer relations side of your business, if you have an excellent business idea and the technical know-how to make that idea a success, if you have the bank manager in the palm of your hand and all the capital you need, but are still worried because you are absolutely hopeless at office administration, you would be well advised to get yourself a partner. In practice, somebody as administratively hopeless as that is unlikely to have the business idea and the marketing skills either, and is probably unlikely to be reading this book at all.

RECEIPTS										PAYMENTS														
Sales Inv. No.	Date	Details	Ref.	Total	VAT	Net Sales	Gross Bank			Date	Details	Ref.	Gross Bank	VAT	Net	Stock/ Materials	Wages	Gas Electric	Rent Rates Insur		Sundries	Drawings		Capital

The analysed cash book

Two rules apply, and if you want to keep things running as smoothly and as simply as possible you would do well to engrave them on your memory: the first is that you must always keep all purchase invoices, all receipts, all documentation of any kind; the second is that you must if at all possible set aside a few minutes each day to enter these transactions into your book. If you do that, you will not be far wrong, and even if you forget you will be all right as long as you have kept everything. The less work your accountant has to do in sorting out all this paperwork, though, the less he or she is going to charge you, so it pays you to keep things up to date, as well as making it easier for you to see how the business is getting on.

How do you start with your accounts? First, open a business bank account. Everything will be far simpler if you can manage to use only your business account for business purposes, and your personal account for personal matters. If you are using part of your house as an office, you are best off paying relevant bills such as electricity and telephone through the business account, and asking your accountant to agree with the tax inspector what proportion of such expenditure relates to the business. It may be another argument for getting separate premises.

In most small businesses, your primary need will be an analysed cash book (see p. 86), available from any good stationer. By this we simply mean a book set out in columns, so that you can set out all financial transactions, whether sales or purchases; use facing pages in the same book if you like. The principle is simple: put the date in the first column, the name of the person the money was received from or paid to in the second. The example shows one way of doing this, with an optional reference to separate sales or purchase ledgers; bank columns provide a helpful check on actual changes in your bank account.

Ideally, it is not enough to write down the details of each cheque you send off, or every time you buy a hundred stamps from the post office; at the end of each month, you need to reconcile your books with your bank statements, ticking off the receipts or withdrawals which appear. That way you can ensure that you include any regular standing orders or direct debits in your accounts as well, and of course that you do not forget bank charges and interest on the overdraft. After that, any cash-book items remaining unticked will be cheques you have sent or received, but which have not yet been cleared. It should be a simple matter to agree the balance in your cash book with the balance on your bank statement. Again, your accountant will be perfectly well able to do this for you, but it makes sense to reconcile your own books to save time and to make sure that you are aware of all the costs of your business, not just the ones you physically deal with.

In addition, you will see from the example that you can analyse your expenditure by category, using a series of subject headings which should differentiate between any major and regular categories, leaving a column of 'sundry expenses' for less important matters. At the bottom of each page, you can total up the figures in each column, so that at the end of each accounting period the running totals will form the basis of the expenditure side of your income and expenditure account. Unless you do this, you will find it difficult to keep a track of how much you have spent on advertising, for example, in a three-month period.

On the receipts side of the equation, you may not need to do more than note the customer name and invoice number, together with a separate column for VAT charged if you are registered; you would, however, probably need a separate column for non-sales income, such as the sale of redundant equipment. If your business sells a number of different products or services, you may also wish to analyse your income to take this into account, and so that you can see where you have room for sales improvement. On the payments side, you will need to make sure that direct costs (labour and materials) are clearly set out independently from overhead costs such as rent, electricity, or telephone expenses; you will remember from the profit and loss account that you must retain a distinction between gross and net profit. Indeed, one of the advantages of the business plan is that it will have familiarized you with a number of these accounting concepts and so enabled you to cope with the day-to-day business administration without too much of a struggle.

Remember too that you will need a separate drawings column for payments for yourself: these must be entered in the books just like any other transaction. When you receive cash from a customer, do not pocket it and spend it on beer and sandwiches; always bank it and record it in the cash book. If you do not do this, your books will not add up, and you could even find yourself in trouble with the Inland Revenue or the Customs and Excise.

When you pay for something, get a receipt, and file the receipts in date order, making sure each has been entered in the cash book. There will of course be times when it is impossible or very difficult to obtain a receipt, and you may need a separate notebook to jot down these items of petty cash expenditure (tube or bus fares are an obvious example). But do try to keep the notebook up to date, or you will find it impossible to remember the precise amounts involved a day or two later. It is generally best to minimize such expenditure by having a business account with the firms you use regularly – stationers, printers, minicabs. That way you can receive an invoice every month and not have to worry too much. The petty cash should be kept in a lockable tin; a float of £50 or so should be enough, with a regular check between the cash book (from which the money has been taken) and your notebook (your petty cash account) to make sure that everything reconciles.

The cash book has only been interested in actual money changing hands. What do you do about purchases you have made, but which have not yet been paid for? Perhaps the purchase was made on credit, and you will receive an invoice in due course; perhaps you have received the invoice, but make it a policy to pay all such bills at the end of the month? As soon as you receive a purchase invoice from another firm, check that the details are correct and that you have indeed received the goods or services you are being charged for. Next, it is probably easiest to keep the current month's invoices together in a folder, in date order. When you pay them all at the end of the month (or whenever you decide is the most convenient moment) you simply enter the details on the payments side of the analysed cash book, together with the cheque number as a reference in each case. You may also like to give each invoice your own number, and file them as they are paid, in date order and in a stronger and more permanent box file.

A similar system can be operated for your sales. As you have seen, the cash book need include little more than the date the money was received, the name of the person or company you sold your product or service to, and the amount banked. But you need to keep track of invoices you send out, and especially of any longstanding debts, so that reminder letters can be sent out after a given period, for example. If you do not do this, you are bound to find that some customers take liberties with an adverse effect on your cash flow.

All you have to do is file your copy of each sales invoice, once again in date and number order; as each customer pays you, you mark the relevant invoice 'paid', enter the appropriate payment in the receipts side of the cash book, and remove the invoice copy to a permanent file. It should go without saying that you bank receipts as soon as is humanly possible. You may, however, find it useful to file unpaid invoices by month, so that you have an immediate check on their age, and can take steps to deal with any which are more than three months old.

A sales ledger is a good idea, especially if you have a relatively small number of good customers for whom you work and bill regularly. All it means is that each customer has his or her own page in the ledger. On the left-hand side (Debit) you note the date the sale was made, what was sold and the amount, together with the sales invoice number; on the right-hand side (Credit) you note all receipts from that customer by date, with a reference to the cash book. In this way, you can keep track of how much a particular customer owes you at any one time, and, in the case of longstanding debts, decide whether you should continue working for that customer.

In a simple business, where transactions are relatively few in number, a well-analysed cash book should be all you really need, though you may find you must use different pages for different accounts, depending on how many columns you have to set up. It may well be worth your while paying for an initial consultation with an accountant, to discuss exactly which accounting systems you are going to need, and which if any of the commercially produced books would be most suitable for your purpose. It will save running into difficulties later, if, for example, you retain large quantities of stock, and feel you may need to account for this separately.

You may have noticed the dread words 'Debit' and 'Credit' appear in the paragraph concerned with the sales ledger. Do not let it worry you. You may not even need a sales ledger if most of your customers are one-off purchasers, and even if you do, there is no need to think of the references to corresponding entries in the cash book as examples of the double-entry system, though that is in effect what they are. For most small businesses of the type discussed in this book, there will be no need to operate a full-scale double-entry book-keeping system; for those who feel they would love to know more (!) there are plenty of excellent courses available. If you get to the stage where accounting systems of that complexity are required, you will almost certainly benefit from employing a part-time, experienced bookkeeper.

Using your accounts

When you put together your business plan, you drew up a projected profit and loss account and cash-flow forecast for the first year of trading. Now that you are starting to trade you want to monitor your actual business performance against those projections, to see where you are doing better or worse than expected, and what action can or should be taken in the light of those conclusions. How do you do it?

The first thing to do is to break down those yearly projections for income and expenditure into monthly totals (see p. 92). Your cash-flow forecast will give you the projected monthly figures for sales and different categories of expenditure, which may well differ from month to month, but which will of course add up to the yearly totals you started with. Now set out those figures for each month in columns, detailing each category of income and expenditure and leaving a second column blank in each case; this will enable you to fill in the

YEAR

	JAN		FEB		MAR		APR		MAY		JUN		JUL		AUG		SEP		OCT		NOV		DEC		TOTAL	
	Budget	Actual	Budget	Actual	Budget	Actual	Budget	Actual	Budget	Actual	Budget	Actual	Budget	Actual	Budget	Actual	Budget	Actual	Budget	Actual	Budget	Actual	Budget	Actual	Budget	Actual
Sales																										
Net purchases																										
Stock & materials																										
Gross profit																										
Rent and rates																										
Insurance																										
Power																										
Heat and light																										
Salaries & NIC																										
Print and stationery																										
Travel																										
Post and telephone																										
Maintenance																										
Advertising																										
Carriage and packing																										
Motor expenses																										
Professional fees																										
Lease/hire purchase																										
Bank charges																										
Interest (loan)																										
Depreciation																										
Total expenditure																										
Net profit																										
Variance																										

Monthly income and expenditure account

actual monthly figures as they emerge and compare them with your projections. The example makes this crystal clear, but the important thing is that you use the figures when they appear, and act on them. If you find your projected sales figures are just not materializing, what are the reasons for the shortfall and what are you going to do about it? You cannot afford to carry on trading just hoping that something will turn up; problems must be identified and rectified, or at least ameliorated: it may be that actual sales figures could still lead to profitability if you reduce your costs elsewhere, so make sure you do.

You can now do exactly the same with your cash-flow forecast, which will be easier since you already have the figures in monthly form. When you have the first month's figures, and a revised cash surplus or deficit, you may find it helpful to revise the projections for the next three months, taking into account this new starting-point. This is known as a 'rolling cash-flow forecast'; it helps you to anticipate problems well in advance, and, for example, marshal your arguments for needing an extra loan if appropriate.

It is a good idea to draw up a fuller profit and loss account after each quarterly period. To do this you will of course need to take into account the value of any stock held at the beginning and end of the period in question. Assuming that there are no direct labour costs involved in the process, the formula can be expressed simply as follows:

(sales + closing stock) − (purchases + opening stock) = gross profit

From that gross profit you will go on to deduct all your other expenses, just as you did when you drew up the projected profit and loss account for the business plan. You may find it helpful to group some of these other expenses: selling and distribution costs (like advertising and transport) could be lumped together separately from administration costs (like rent and electricity). And remember to include the depreciation of any capital equipment.

Ultimately, how you use your accounts is up to you; you must find the system best suited to your needs, and stick to it. It cannot be repeated too often that accounts are not sent to try you, but for you to use for you own benefit, to improve the efficiency and profitability of your business. Make sure you are in control.

This mention of control leads quite naturally to the question of computers, which many people seem to regard as a means of taking all such worries away from them, as if the computer would keep the books up to date automatically. But the old adage 'Garbage in, garbage out' is just as valid as ever, and if you do not really understand your accounts in the first place, a computer will make things worse and not better, because you will now have to understand the computer as well. Computerization of accounts can indeed pay dividends when you are an established company with a large number of transactions to add up, and a series of double-entry books which need simplifying. But such a process is a long way off when you are starting out, and is best forgotten for the time being.

Professional advice is another matter, and even if you are a sole trader you would be well advised to employ a chartered accountant to draw up your end of year accounts, partly so that you know your tax and VAT returns have been properly compiled, but, just as important, so that you know that your figures are accurate. If you have followed the systems described above, and kept your own books up to date, the accountant's fees need not be astronomical. Personal recommendation is still the best means of finding any professional adviser, but in the absence of business friends in the locality, you can obtain a list of chartered accountants in your district by writing to the Institute of Chartered Accountants. Then contact a few of these, outlining the kind of work you do and asking them whether they have experience of dealing with small businesses in this field.

Making sure you get paid

This section will assume that you are not in the lucky position of being paid in advance, or in a business such as hairdressing, when you are paid on the spot. Being in one of those situations does not of course mean that you should neglect any of the elementary accounting principles, but at least those financial problems you do run into should not be the result of bad debts.

It is a different matter when you invoice your customers or clients after the completion of the work. A company selling television sets can in the last resort repossess the television from a non-paying customer, but if you are, say, an electrician who has recently rewired a factory, you can hardly go in and rip out your own handiwork. In addition to this, you will have had to pay for the cost of materials yourself already, and you may have had to pay for the cost of other labour. What do you do?

One short answer is to insist that you are always paid at least a portion of your estimated charge for the job in advance; by doing this, you might at the very least cover the cost of materials and hence ensure that you are not actually out of pocket. Similarly, you might only work for people who are able to provide references to other local businesses they have used. But in the real competitive business world, you may be very reluctant to turn down a lucrative job, especially when you are trying to establish yourself. And some of the worst offenders in the slow payment stakes are in any case larger companies with excellent reputations, who simply delay payment as long as possible as a matter of accounting policy.

There are, however, a number of principles you ought to follow. For a start, do make sure you bill your customer as soon as you have completed the contract; there is no advantage to you in letting the invoices build up before you take them to the post office. And make sure the invoice is correct: it may seem a niggling point, but any inaccuracy, even in the matter of calculation of VAT, for example, only gives an excuse for the customer to delay payment further by querying the bill.

After a month, make a polite inquiry to the customer or their accounts department, stressing that you are a little concerned about things getting lost, and want to clarify the situation. After another month you can afford to be less charming, but still polite; if you are still engaged in work for the customer, explain that with the best will in the world you cannot go on like this. After three months it is time to get tough. Perhaps you have offered to accept payment by instalments but no money has yet arrived; you have certainly had enough of this troublesome customer and made a private decision not to do business with him or her again. What legal threats can you initiate?

There is normally no need to go through a solicitor or a debt collecting agency, unless the amount in dispute is very large and, for example, the quality of your work is being questioned. All you need do is write a firm but polite letter, along the following lines:

> Dear Sir/Madam
>
> We note that we have received no response to our letters of 3 March and 2 April 1989 requesting payment for the consultancy services we provided in December 1988 and January 1989 (our invoice number: 1372). We now wish to give notice that unless we receive full payment of the outstanding debt of £475 within the next fourteen days, we shall begin proceedings in the County Court without further notice.
>
> Yours faithfully

The reference to the County Court in this instance is to the Small Claims Division, where claims worth less than £500 can be heard informally without legal representation and at minimal cost. Your County Court will be able to advise you on how to issue a summons; ask for copies of two government publications: *Small claims in the county court* and *Enforcing money judgments in the county court*. In practice, it is obviously in everybody's interest not to have to go to this much trouble and your threatening letter will in many cases have the desired effect of getting the customer to pay you. Even if he or she only pays you part of what is owed, and offers the remainder in instalments, you should still accept; bringing a court case for the full amount will not produce the desired effect if the other side is simply unable to pay, and the court itself will in any case almost certainly allow the defendant to pay off the debt in a series of instalments.

It is vital that you retain copies of any correspondence you have had with the customer concerned, together with invoices, receipts and any other documentation relating to the transaction. If you do find yourself in court, you will need to be able to prove the facts of the case and you cannot do that without the paperwork. For the same reason, always behave reasonably, whether you are writing a letter or paying a personal visit to the recalcitrant customer. If your correspondence is produced in court and found to contain threatening phrases or even obscenities, you are not going to create that all-important impression of being long-suffering and eminently reasonable. If you are in the right, it does not make sense for you to give your customer any means of getting back at you. The same, of course, applies to the quality of the work you do, and your adherence to any contractual obligations.

The problems that small businesses face as a result of slow payment must be taken very seriously. Remarkably, recent research shows that such businesses wait an average of 75 days from the date of invoice for payment. Just think about that for a minute. When you drew up your cash-flow forecast, how long did you assume that your customers would take to pay you? Few people would think in terms of more than a month, and certainly not 75 days. Of course, that is an average figure, and you must make sure that you are not in that position; if you are, it should be obvious by now what sort of effect that is going to have on your cash flow and on your ability to keep trading.

A general consensus is emerging among politicians, lawyers, trade associations and business lobby groups such as the Forum of Private Business that voluntary codes of practice are inadequate given the scale of this problem, and that Parliament ought to legislate, perhaps to allow businesses to charge interest on overdue invoices. Supporters of the campaign point out sourly that the government is quite prepared to legislate to ensure that businesses pay their VAT or corporation tax.

In the meantime, the Small Firms Division of the Department of

Employment has produced a booklet entitled *Prompt Payment Please* as a guide to businesses which are suffering. The philosophy behind it is that good credit management is vital; unless you know who owes you money, how much they owe you, and how long they have owed it, you are in a weak position when it comes to doing something about those debts. Remember that securing payment of old debts is just as important as finding new business: there is not a lot of point in having huge sales figures, if half of the resultant income has never actually been received. To that extent, you can do a lot to help yourself, simply by making sure you have the right attitude.

And that is really the second point the Department is emphasizing in its booklet: have the right attitude, take a firm line with the bullies. They are in the wrong, you are in the right, do not apologize to anybody for claiming what is yours. Even if you lose one or two customers in the short term, you may find that your reputation for not putting up with any nonsense stands you in good stead, and means that you are paid in advance of other creditors who are less pressing. Who wants a reputation for being a soft touch? Be persistent: if a firm says they are about to put a cheque in the post, keep telephoning them until they get so fed up with you they really do put the cheque in the post. It works wonders.

The other side of the coin, of course, is that you too may wish to delay payment for purchases you have made if you find yourself without cash for a short period. If this keeps happening, have a good look at your accounts again, and see whether you have borrowed enough to withstand temporary fluctuations in cash flow. Some things are easier to avoid paying than others – generally, you will find that government bodies, banks and finance companies, British Telecom and your electricity board are the most pressing, in the last two instances simply because they have the power to cut you off. But even here, you can nearly always negotiate a stay of execution if you agree to pay off the debt in instalments within a reasonable space of time.

Understanding VAT

It is true that VAT inspectors have draconian powers, true too that most types of business discussed in this book will need to register. But there is really no need to panic. As with so many seemingly frightening aspects of business life, coping with VAT is chiefly a question of keeping accurate records, and keeping them up to date. As long as you have all the paperwork, you can in the last resort go to a professional accountant and ask him to relieve you of the burden of your quarterly VAT return. That is the worst that can possibly happen, even if you find the whole thing totally incomprehensible.

But once again, there is really no reason why you should not be quite capable of preparing your own VAT returns, and accounting for VAT along with all of your other transactions. As with everything else, you simply need to grasp a few basic principles, and the time to do that is before you start trading, not when your first VAT return is due.

First of all you must decide whether the products or services you are selling will be exempt from VAT, zero-rated, or subject to VAT at the standard rate (currently 15 per cent). If you are involved in insurance, or in betting, or in providing medical services, you will be exempt, but such fields are unlikely to concern many readers of this book. Zero-rating will affect more: exports are zero-rated, together with food (but not catering), books and newspapers, and children's clothing and footwear, for example. From this it will already be apparent that the category each type of business falls into is something of a mystery, and if you are in any doubt at all you would be well advised to take professional advice, either from your accountant, or from HM Customs and Excise, who will send you copies of free leaflets giving you the up-to-date position, with titles like *Should I be Registered for VAT?*

If you are exempt from VAT, you need not and indeed cannot register. It may come as something of a surprise to many, but exemption is usually seen as a disadvantage: your purchases from other businesses will still be subject to VAT, which you will still have to pay, but which you will not be able to claim back. Operating a business in which most or all of your products or services are zero-rated, on the other hand, will almost certainly be an advantage; you will be able to claim back VAT you are charged, without having to charge any VAT to your own customers. This may well mean that every quarter you will receive a nice little cheque from HM Customs and Excise in repayment of VAT you have been charged, and in practice they will probably encourage you to apply for exemption. Whether you do this or not depends on how much you hate preparing the quarterly VAT return, and how much money you are recovering on each occasion; it may also depend on how confident you are about your ability to keep your books in order, since somebody in this happy position is almost certain to find his or her VAT returns subject to closer scrutiny.

Whether or not you must register is also dependent on the turnover of your business. The threshold increases every year, but in 1989–90 you must register if your annual turnover is over £23,600. This will obviously be true of most small businesses, and in practice you are well advised to register if your turnover is likely to be anywhere near this; it will save problems later, if you find you go over the threshold after all. The need for this is emphasized by the fact that there is also a lower limit for any one quarter, which means that if your annual turnover is £15,000, but you earn £10,000 in July, August and September, you will still have to register, at least initially, and then convince Customs and Excise that your annual turnover will still be below the higher limit.

To register, you get the form VAT 1 from Customs and Excise. The date of registration, which you state on the form, is the date from which you first had reasonable grounds to believe your turnover would exceed £23,600. For a new business, this may well be the day you started to trade, and it is possible to reclaim VAT you were charged in setting up your business. As soon as you know you are required to be registered, you must start accounting for VAT, even if this is before you receive your VAT registration number. One important point to note is that you cannot show VAT as a separate item on an invoice until you have received your registration number; if you need to charge VAT in this early period, you must simply adjust your price, and then explain to any customers who are themselves registered that you will send them tax invoices later.

What records do you need to keep? You are of course required to keep all invoices and credit notes you issue or receive; if you export goods or services, you will need to have evidence of this available, such as Customs documentation. You are required to keep VAT accounts, showing on the one hand the VAT you have been charged on purchases, and on the other hand the VAT you have charged on your own sales.

As we have seen, for small businesses with a relatively small number of financial transactions, such data can be included in your analysed cash book along with other income and expenditure. At the end of the quarter for which the VAT return is required, you can add up the totals from the columns. With the help of the Customs and Excise leaflet *Filling in Your VAT Return* you will need to draw up a VAT reconciliation statement, as in the illustration. The reason for this is that VAT is normally accounted for at the date of the invoice, not when the money is actually received: by keeping your sales and purchase invoices in order, as the first section of this chapter set out, you should be able to add or subtract figures for debtors or creditors without too much difficulty. You will also note that before you enter the figures for output (sales) and input (purchases) you will need to deduct certain items such as salaries and insurance. Again, this is not too difficult, providing you have analysed your cash book in the correct way, have retained all invoices in order, and have the leaflet in front of you to help. The first time you do this, you may want to make a copy of the form first so that you can make a mess of it without having to worry. And always remember that you can seek advice on anything you are not clear about; even VAT inspectors are surprisingly human.

VAT is inevitably harder on businesses which make a large number of sales direct to the public, sales which fall into different categories; if this means you, you may be able to take advantage of the special retail schemes which exist, so ask your local VAT office. Since 1 October 1987 it has also been possible to join a Cash Accounting Scheme, which simplifies matters by making the VAT payable or receivable the difference between VAT on payments actually received and actually made; in this way you are not reduced to paying VAT on bad debts you may never receive. Finally, on 1 July 1988 these schemes were joined by the Annual Accounting Scheme, enabling certain businesses to pay nine monthly instalments of VAT based on the previous year's assessment, and only complete one annual VAT return, which then becomes a balancing statement; however, there are certain requirements you must satisfy before joining this scheme (you are ineligible if you regularly receive payments of VAT, for example).

VAT will only take over your business if you let it; if it is getting on top of you, seek advice, either from Customs and Excise or from your accountant. It is not worth struggling with.

Tax returns

In this section we will be assuming that you are a sole trader, and therefore self-employed for tax purposes. If you are a director of a limited company, you will be an employee and your tax dealt with through the PAYE system along with any other employee. Your company may also be subject to corporation tax on any profits it makes, but since you will have to have your annual accounts audited by a chartered accountant, you can trust him or her to deal with that for you.

If you are self-employed, you may also wish to entrust the filing of your tax returns to your accountant, but it will be to your benefit to have some idea of the principles behind taxation in this country. If you run a business as a sole trader, you will be taxed on any profits that business makes, regardless of how much you have actually drawn from the business account for your own use. But your big advantage is that you are not taxed on the gross income, but on the income after all allowable business expenses have been deducted.

Again, your accountant will give you advice on what is likely to be accepted, and should give you that advice before you start trading, to help with the day-to-day accounting procedures. But here are some examples. If you go out for a meal with your spouse, or indeed with one of your customers, you would be best advised to pay with your personal rather than your business cheque book, since entertainment is not a tax-deductible expense unless the recipient is an employee on the PAYE system or an overseas customer. If you are running the business from home, you would be able to claim a reasonable proportion of expenses such as rates and electricity, but if you do you could run into capital gains tax problems when you sell the house. Another argument for entirely separate premises, perhaps.

Other expenses are much clearer, and should be straightforward if you keep your business and personal paperwork separate: raw materials, advertising, postage, stationery, telephone, financial charges such as interest on a loan, professional fees, subs to trade associations and staff wages should cause you no problems. Business travel is allowable, but not for the journey between home and work; again, if your car is used for business *and* domestic purposes, you will need to apportion between them. Clothing is allowable if it is essential for your business (such as protective wear), but not otherwise. Pension schemes are an excellent idea for the self-employed because of the tax relief they attract, but probably best left until you are a little more established.

Capital expenditure is treated rather differently, and you may be able to claim allowances depending on what the expenditure was for and whether you paid on a hire-purchase or leased basis. Here it will be essential to seek professional advice.

When do you pay the Inland Revenue? The first point is that you do not have to notify anybody that you have set up a business until after the end of the first year of trading (that is, the period from when you commence until the following 4 April). It is in your interest to set up your business as soon as possible after the previous 5 April; that way you need not pay any income tax for nearly a year. In general, you pay income tax on your past, not your current, earnings, which is obviously a considerable advantage, provided that your profits continue to increase. If you have the money, it is a good idea to keep future tax liabilities firmly in mind and even to put money aside in a deposit account for this purpose, though this will not be possible if you are operating on an overdraft.

You must, of course, also pay your flat Class 2 National Insurance contributions, either by weekly stamp or direct debit; additional Class 4 contributions may be assessed on your profits and collected by the Inland Revenue at the same time as your income tax.

Expanding and taking on staff

There is no point in your taking on a full-time or even part-time employee if you only really need extra help occasionally; if you need casual labour, you are better off giving one of your friends or a member of your family the chance to earn a bit extra over a weekend or a couple of evenings. You may well find that in your first year of operation you will be able to do without any more than this.

Similarly, you may pass through that period in the life of most small businesses when you have more work than you can comfortably take care of, but not enough to justify the employment of extra staff. If this happens to you, you can do little other than work still harder in generating still more work, so that you can afford extra staff. You might also be able to get your partner or one of your children to help out with the paperwork, on a voluntary basis. But what happens when you are doing so well that you decide you can afford the extra labour?

Even here, you need to think about precisely what you need before you charge off to the Jobcentre or advertise in the local rag. Do you need a skilled person, another bricklayer or electrician or plumber for example? If you do, you will clearly have to pay local market rates; perhaps you would prefer to take on a school-leaver, and give him or her some work experience? If you do this, you should be mindful that if the employee gets a taste for the kind of work, he or she may well leave you after a few months to seek a more formal training opportunity in a larger firm. Make sure you know precisely what you need, and what you can afford, before you enter the recruitment arena.

Jobcentres are free; recruitment agencies charge you a fat percentage of the annual wage you are paying the recruit. Against that, specialist agencies are more likely to attract candidates of a higher calibre and will not waste your time sending you unsuitable people to interview. In general, an agency will only be a better bet if you are looking for skills and experience.

If you advertise, it is of course illegal to specify that you want an 'English' person or a 'young man'; any such descriptions offend legislation against race or sex discrimination. If you have an exact description in your mind of the kind of person you are looking for, then by all means make your advertisement as specific in its requirements as possible, to avoid time-wasting; on the other hand, try not to be too dismissive of any applicants who fall, for example, outside your preferred age range – your own preconceived ideal may be too narrow and risk missing an otherwise excellent candidate. Remember that if you want your employee to stay with you and provide an element of stability to your growing business, an older person is more likely to do that.

Depending on the kind of work you do, you may prefer to have an initial telephone chat to assess suitability, or on the other hand ask to see a CV. Before you see anybody, always jot down the questions you want to ask them, and make sure that you are as open as possible about your business and the work you are hoping to employ them for. Give the applicant time to ask questions – that way you can learn a lot about how he or she sees your business and about enthusiasm for the work.

When you appoint anybody to work more than 16 hours per week, you must within 13 weeks provide a written statement detailing their conditions of employment. You would be well advised to get a solicitor to help you in drawing up this document, since there are a number of legal requirements which must be met. The same goes for regulations on questions of health and safety at work, trade union membership, dismissal, and of course your requirement to have employer's liability insurance. Always seek legal advice when in doubt. The Department of Employment produces a comprehensive series of booklets on all aspects of taking on staff; these should be available free from your local Jobcentre or benefit office, and are worth keeping in your office for reference.

You will also have to deduct tax and national insurance contributions from the employee's wages, if earnings are above a certain threshold, in addition to paying the employer's NI contribution. It is not difficult to do this: contact the nearest tax office when you first become an employer, and you will receive all the necessary documents and instructions. Again, if you find these things incomprehensible, your accountant will be pleased to handle your PAYE records for you, but really it is just a matter of keeping accurate records as you go along, like any other aspect of business accounting.

Always listen when your employees present you with grievances or suggestions for improvement. For example, you might have taught each worker how to do a group of small jobs, but never explained why they are important to the business as a whole. If you ensure that everybody understands his or her role within the organization, you develop a sense of worth and also enable the worker to take on new responsibilities much more easily.

The final point about becoming an employer is perhaps the most important. Think back to the decision you made to go it alone; was that decision partly as a result of dissatisfaction with the way you were treated at work in the past? If you are honest with yourself, you may agree that if your employer had given you credit for a good piece of work, had shown an interest in you as a person and what made you tick, had tried to understand the reasons behind your persistent lateness rather than just shouting at you, had given you extra responsibility when it was deserved and even a small share of the profits, then you might have felt much more committed to that employer, much more keen to help out voluntarily in a crisis, much more likely to stay and progress with the company. Most of these things do not cost money, and you may feel they are matters of common sense, but they are none the less surprisingly easy to forget when you are working desperately hard to fulfil a contract deadline.

And what about the broader questions involved in expansion? You may, after all, be quite happy as your own boss, with complete control over the hours you work and the amount of money you bring in. It may not make you a millionaire, but you are confident of continuing to make a living without unnecessary stress. Fine. In general terms, if your interest is primarily in the type of business you are rather than in the concept of business itself, in the work you do for customers rather than the paperwork involved in managing your business, you might be better to stick to what you know and are good at. If, on the other hand, you cannot wait to develop new products and secure ever bigger contracts, if your enthusiasm is for business deals and you look forward to the day when you need no longer get your hands dirty, you are in a rather different category. The key point is that either road is an entirely legitimate one for any small business to take, so do not let anybody browbeat you into doing something you do not want to do.

This book is concerned only with your first year of operation; if you reach the expansion stage, you will need more specialized advice. But a few words (and only a few) should be said about the obverse side of every business coin: what happens if everything goes disastrously wrong?

You should first of all remind yourself of what the first chapter said about setting yourself targets, both in terms of the time required to start earning an acceptable living, and in terms of limiting your financial loss. You must set yourself clear limits, so that when you pass these limits you accept that the business has failed, and decide what you want to do next. One good general rule is to avoid bankruptcy if possible, which simply means that you need to be able to pay off the debts of the business, if necessary from your own resources. Bearing that in mind will give you a rule of thumb as to how long to carry on trading in the hope that business improves, for you must always know how much you personally could afford to lose if the worst came to the worst.

There is no need to end on such a negative note. Even after a business failure, you must try to retain a sense of detachment, try to explain rationally why your business failed to meet its targets – your business plan and financial projections will act as a good starting-point here. Perhaps you gave too much credit too soon and simply ended up with no money in your business account; or perhaps your business idea was inadequately thought out, and the market you confidently projected was simply not there in reality. Whatever you decide, do not blame yourself for the business failure; few even among successful businesses could claim to have lived trouble free. You will have learnt an enormous amount from the experience, and you may already have another idea in the pipeline, though you might need a more conventional period of employment to re-establish your capital base as well as your self-confidence.

But if you really have followed the principles outlined in this book, if you really do have the right idea and the management skills to make that idea a profitable reality, there is no reason why it should come to that.

PART II

101 businesses you can start on £5000 or less

Advertising agency

Formal qualifications are not too important in this business, but a background of work experience in another agency is a must. Confidence in your own ability is a great help in convincing clients that you know what you are talking about, but you must be able to come up with a flow of ideas, even if much of the detailed creative work can be farmed out to freelancers. You need a smart office, possibly in a business centre, and up-to-date office equipment, but otherwise start-up costs need not be great.

The big problem in the early days will be generating business, so it is a great help if you can attract a few clients from your previous agency. Most agencies specialize in particular commercial sectors; the more contacts you have in your chosen fields, the better. You can try a mailshot to likely small or medium-sized firms, but it has to be really good to make an impact; if you cannot sell yourself to the client, you cannot sell the client.

You must keep abreast of the trade magazine *Campaign*, and be constantly looking for new ways of advertising your clients, and new markets to advertise them to.

Ancestry research services

A history degree, or some training in historical research, is useful; experience in researching your own family history, and an enthusiasm for the subject, more important. If you have worked on friends' families as well, so much the better: you need to have an awareness of different sorts of families and problems, so attending an evening class or other group project would be helpful. There is no real professional body, though the Association of Genealogists and Record Agents likes to think of itself as one; if you can get on the list, it might bring you a little extra work, but is unlikely to make the difference between success and failure. The Institute of Heraldic and Genealogical Studies runs courses and hands out diplomas, but again these are not widely recognized, though they may give you more confidence to break out on your own. There are plenty of introductory books (shelved under 929 at the local library); read as many as you can. If you live far from London you may have to be prepared to travel a fair bit so as not to limit yourself to too narrow a geographical patch.

This is a difficult market to pin down, and advertising in the more lavish national magazines with a historical bent (*Heritage, This England, Illustrated London News*) is not cheap. If you are concentrating on a relatively small area, you should find the county magazines a better bet. One important point to remember is that genealogy is a fascinating subject to a lot of people, so it should give you plenty of opportunities for the public relations/press release approach. If you have some famous local personalities, why not offer to trace their ancestry for them and write it up for press consumption? Repeat business and personal recommendation is very important in this kind of work.

Most of your work will come by post, so you should work from home if feasible. Apart from postage, stationery and advertising, you might want a cheap word processor for your client reports. You will need an annual subscription to the Society of Genealogists (£25 or £16, depending on where you live), which maintains an extensive library of reference material. The main research costs will be on travel, and marriage and birth certificates: make sure your clients know that these must be paid for in addition to your own research time. Top researchers command as much as £15 per hour, others charge £5 or less; you will have to judge where your own skills and experience place you on this scale.

Make sure everybody understands at the outset that you are charging for research time, and not for results; if the case is a difficult one, and you discover nothing, you must still be paid. Because of this, it is advisable to secure at least a proportion of the costs upfront.

Antique dealing

Go to antique fairs and markets, to see what is selling where, and whether there are obvious needs not being met. Find out how much it costs to hire stalls in the places you are most interested in; advertisements in local newspapers should give details of opening times and a contact number for the organizer. You may find getting a really good site means a wait, but in this trade location is very important. The *Antiques Trade Gazette* should also be studied for details of forthcoming antique fairs.

You will need to invest at least a few hundred pounds on initial stock; unless you are already really knowledgeable, the best way to do this may be to buy from the rougher end of the market-stall trade and resell in your own more upmarket location; a great deal of trade in this business consists of items being recycled from cheaper to more expensive stall to shop. You will need a garage, or somewhere else to store items while you are not actually selling. Aside from this, antique dealing is the kind of business you can pick up as you go along, though it does no harm to invest in reference books, or talk to other traders about the best locations (choose somebody who is not selling the same things). It is always better to sell something for less than its true value than not to sell it at all. And as you grow in confidence and knowledge, you can visit auctions, clear people's houses (make sure you can get rid of the rubbish as well as the good stuff) and eventually perhaps specialize in Georgian silver or antique toys, opening your own exclusive arcade shop and becoming a pillar of the London and Provincial Antique Dealers' Association.

The Association, or perhaps one of its members, may be prepared to give you some important advice on staying within the law and protecting yourself from stolen goods and fraud. It is a very incestuous business – you have to have one eye constantly fixed on what everybody else is buying and selling, and at what price.

Antique furniture restoration

You need natural skill and a feel for wood to do this work, and you will have to enrol on a course at a local technical college if you have no previous experience. Try contacting the British Antique Furniture Restorers' Association for advice; or you may persuade a dealer to train you or give you some temporary work experience.

You have a choice in terms of the kind of business you want to run: you can offer a service to people, collecting their furniture and returning it restored; or you can buy, restore and sell furniture at a profit. In the latter case, the business is really an offshoot of antique dealing, and most of the same principles apply; in the former, potential customers are not likely to entrust you with their prized possessions unless they have knowledge of your work, so word of mouth is likely to be the most effective means of securing business. If you have taken a recognized course at an adult education institute, you may be able to obtain work from furniture or antique dealers; contact them direct. As with most personal services, speed and efficiency, as well as quality, are ways of giving yourself the edge over your competitors, though there is always a strong demand for a really skilled craftsman. Remember not to overdo the restoration: to many people, there is little point in an antique so pristine that it no longer looks like an antique.

You will need at least a garage or large garden shed, and preferably a warehouse, in which to work surrounded by your inflammable spirits and french polish. Take advice about fire safety measures and insurance. You will also need to spend money on good tools, and have transport available.

Artificial flower making

These can be made from anything from paper to silk or satin. The skill of making them is a largely self-taught craft, and if you are interested you will probably have been making artificial flowers for your own amusement for almost as long as you can remember. If your design and production quality are good enough, you can market to local stores, and of course contact hotels, pubs, conference centres and so on directly. It is very much up to you to create your own market, by convincing potential buyers that your products really do look as good as the real thing. The only way you can do this is by arriving, samples in hand.

Beauty therapy

You must be trained and qualified for this – write first to the National Federation of Beauty Therapists for details of courses and diplomas, which may be privately run or available through adult education institutes or even the London College of Fashion. And you will need to invest some money for electrolysis equipment, for example, as well as cosmetics and skin treatments. If you are going to set yourself up in a salon, you will need a relaxing waiting-room as well as a hygienic and well-equipped room in which to treat your clients. You will also probably need to employ a receptionist. Because of such capital outlay, you might prefer to offer a travelling service (similar to a hairdresser) and visit people in their own homes; they may be more relaxed about the treatment there in any case. But if so, you will need a reliable vehicle and be prepared to build in travel costs. You will also need liability insurance against any injuries you may cause your clients.

All in all, this is not a cheap or an easy option, but there is potential for high earnings among those who can afford to pay for such services. You might be able to market yourself via the more expensive local hairdressers, or even through glossy magazines if these have a high circulation in your area, or if you are prepared to travel some distance. Otherwise, word of mouth is probably going to bring you a high proportion of your work.

Bed and breakfast

This is only likely to be lucrative if you live in a major tourist centre where the demand for accommodation far outstrips the supply, and have a large house with plenty of spare bedrooms. In general, you may only let 50 per cent of your bedrooms to guests (so, for example, if you own a four-bedroom house, you may install tourists in two bedrooms). There are further restrictions: the rooms you let must not be basement or attic rooms, and fire exits will have to be provided. If you do not own the house, your landlord will have to provide permission for your business activities. Your premiums for home contents insurance are bound to increase once you give house keys to strangers.

You would be advised to contact your local Tourist Authority at the outset, both for advice on such legal points and also as your principal marketing tool; unless you are on the approved list of accommodation, you will not be able to reach many tourists. Of course, if you install a luxury private bathroom and television in every room, you will be able to have your facilities graded more highly and hence charge more, but you may first prefer to test the water without too much capital outlay.

Bed manufacturing

There is a large demand for the four-poster, from hotels in particular, but if you are interested in this kind of business there is no point in trying to compete with the manufacturers of reproduction models; you must undertake to restore and rebuild originals, and as such your business is really a branch of antique furniture restoration; most of the same principles (including the qualifications needed) will apply. You will need to combine the knowledge to spot and buy genuine bedposts and bedends with the skill to make the frames and canopies, and of course appropriate curtains; you will also need to offer a delivery and erection service.

An initial direct mailshot may be worthwhile to make contact with potential buyers; after that repeat business will be your major concern. If you are selling large beds at £2000 or more each, you are not going to have to (or indeed, to be able to) make and sell very many each month.

Bicycle repairs

This is not going to make you rich, but there is an ever-increasing interest in cycling as a healthier means of travel, and a bicycle is now a valuable piece of machinery worth repairing and servicing. There are plenty of books about bikes, and it should go without saying that you will be an enthusiast with experience of maintaining your own models. You will need a garage or perhaps a large garden shed – somewhere you can work under cover, anyway, and somewhere which is secure at night. You will need to invest a certain amount in tools – spanners of all shapes and sizes, tyre levers, soldering kit and so on – though you may well possess most of these already.

Put advertisements in newsagents' windows initially, then expand by advertising in the local press. Charge an hourly rate, but always remember to add on the cost of materials (negotiate bulk deals with a bike shop). When you become well known, you can broaden the base of your business by buying up old machines, renovating them, and selling them at a good profit.

Boat repairs

If you live in a boating centre, and have some nautical college training, for example, you might consider a business in this field. You will need to spend capital on the rent of a good-sized workshop, and plenty of equipment, including perhaps a portable generator, water pump, and shot blaster. If you have good contacts in the local sailing world, you should be able to secure plenty of repair contracts.

This may sound a bit too much like a certain TV soap opera, but there is money to be made in boats, and if you can go into partnership with a designer you might even end up piloting and manufacturing your own models.

Bookbinding

This is skilled work, but courses are available, and so is plenty of work. You do not need a great deal of space, so a room in your house, or at least a shed or garage, would be a possibility. You do need to buy tools, such as a powered guillotine. As ever, an understanding of your local market is crucial; the lion's share of your business is likely to come from bulk orders from schools or churches for the rebinding of textbooks or hymnals, rather than those one-off seventeenth-century priceless leather tomes. But that does not mean that you cannot develop a craft side to your business by, for example, making your own attractively bound notepads and diaries for sale as gifts in nearby tourist centres.

Book-keeping

You will have some employment experience in accounting, and a good knowledge of the double-entry system, and of accounting for VAT. Or perhaps you have taken one of the many available courses. Although all accounting systems are based on the same principles, most of the businesses or individuals you will be working for will have their own ways of doing things, and these you will be expected to adhere to. You will need a desk, a filing cabinet and perhaps copies of up-to-date tax legislation, but such a business can easily be operated from home, as long as confidential business records are securely locked away. You might need transport to carry heavy files back and forth, and you may be required to provide the stationery for each job, so learn where to buy in bulk.

The best marketing approach is likely to be direct, to local small businesses. Go in person, because busy people will not answer speculative letters. Try to offer references: if you can persuade bank managers, accountants and solicitors to recommend you, so much the better. Charges will vary depending on experience, but you might think at the outset in terms of an hourly rate akin to what a qualified secretary would be paid. You could charge more if you are able to offer computer skills; this is likely to become almost essential as more and more firms computerize their transactions.

Initially, you may be luckiest with businesses whose accounts are in a terrible mess and who need somebody to take them away and put them in order; once you have done this, the businesses might prefer you to visit their premises for a couple of hours a week to keep things up to date.

Bookmaking

If you want to be a bookie you will be well advised to start by working for one of the big four betting chains, who give on-the-job training. Needless to say, your mental arithmetic must be excellent, and you must have an awareness of the regulations maintained by the Gaming Board.

The best way of entering the business without much capital is to get an annual permit to operate on a racecourse; all you really need is a blackboard on which you chalk the odds, and a car to get you between courses. You need to have a detailed awareness of animals' form, but probably more important is the mental agility to keep ahead of your competitors in a fast-moving situation.

It is really impossible to predict how much you will lose or make in this business, but if you have a flair for it you will realize very quickly.

Bookselling (mail order)

Forget all about opening a bookshop, however much you like the idea: it requires too much capital, and profit margins are not high enough to allow for the stock you will inevitably buy and be unable to sell. The problem with selling books is that each title is really a market all of its own; it follows that the only way to make money is to reduce the number of titles you sell to manageable limits, and to sell only those titles for which you know you have a ready buyer or buyers.

One answer is to sell secondhand books by mail order, sending out a catalogue several times a year to anybody who has bought a book from you previously or who you think might be interested. Specialize in a subject – history is a very obvious one – and buy up anything saleable in that field: this will include the recent academic monographs often readily found in university towns as well as the kind of antiquarian book often bought more for its plates than for its text. By offering such a specialist service, you can obtain top prices, since the customer is making big savings in time and convenience. You will know a lot about your chosen field, and will have friends and acquaintances willing to buy books from you; get them to suggest other names, and the list should snowball quite effectively. After a while you can buy unwanted books from your customers, as well as more obvious sources: auctions, secondhand shops, student noticeboards.

Your catalogue must be well produced and informative about the books and their condition; ask some booksellers for samples to see how it is done, and how you can improve on the competition.

Building (general)

One of the most traditional of all small-business openings, but none the less valid. You will have been apprenticed to a building trade – bricklaying, joinery, plastering – and have good general skills besides your own speciality. You may want to go into business with a colleague, or alternatively have a network of self-employed contacts you can employ for short periods as necessary. The building trade is competitive; you need to have a very precise idea of what other local businesses are offering, and what they are charging. You really do need a 'unique selling proposition'; with the widespread fear of cowboys an emphasis on quality work, backed up with impressive references, is as good a way to start as any. You will need at least a reliable van and your own basic tools, but you can trade from home provided that you are not upsetting the neighbours with a steady stream of heavy lorries and deliveries.

Start with extensions and similar small jobs, if you have an entrepreneurial flair you will sooner or later be tempted into buying and doing up property, but this is not so lucrative as it once was, since even the most neglected properties in desirable areas tend to fetch surprisingly high prices. In any case, this is something to consider only when you have built up enough of a business to be able to borrow larger capital sums.

Business history

Some experience of historical research and writing is important, but so is an understanding of how business has always operated; you need to know how to read the ledgers and minute books of the past as much as the broader history of the kind of industry the firm was involved in. Interviewing skills, and ability to inspire trust, are also important; the more business contacts you have, the better. Read *Business History*, a booklet originally published by the Historical Association and updated by Debrett's Business History Research Ltd in 1984. And read as many business histories as you can lay your hands on, especially the shorter and well-illustrated ones.

Large companies in the market for a business history are going to employ an established author on a full-time basis; there is no point in your trying to compete. Your market must be small businesses in your locality, or in industries you have specialist knowledge of. There is no point in journal advertising, though it is certainly worth writing about yourself in as many trade journals as you can. Beyond this, direct mail is the way forward; always follow up with a telephone call a few days later, and make the most of any personal connection you have with the business. Solicitors and other professional advisers may be particularly valuable clients to have, because they can refer you to other potential buyers. Remember that a company does not have to be two hundred years old to be of interest; even after thirty years a business has an interesting story to tell, and telling that story in illustrated brochure form can be an important marketing tool, emphasizing stability and permanence.

You will visit your clients on their premises, so you should not need an office. However, you do need an excellent brochure, good-quality stationery and a good typewriter/word processor; presentation is very important. It is up to you whether you simply prepare a written report and leave the client to decide on the form of publication, or whether you can also arrange for design and printing; the latter service could obviously add substantially to your income. You will probably agree an all-inclusive fee; think in terms of a research period of, say, a month, when negotiating this.

It is very important to agree your parameters with your client at the outset; every business will have confidential material it does not want to publicize, and you must respect this. Companies will of course vary in how much freedom they give you to criticize past performance, or previous employees; again, this is something you must sort out before you begin. It will be best to agree regular progress meetings with one or two senior client staff, to iron out any difficulties.

Cab driving

One of the traditional ways of making money for the self-employed, often on a casual basis. There is always a demand for drivers with their own four-door cars, and if you have no previous experience you would be well advised to work for an existing firm first. That way you can assess the competition and the profit margins and try to identify a gap in the market.

When you are running your own business the major problem will be to attract drivers, unless you have a large extended family to serve as a base for your operations. Make sure that all your drivers have clean licences, sound cars and proper hire insurance. You will have to supply a radio phone to each driver, for which you will receive rent. A cheap office above a shop may be all you need to begin with, but telephone bills will be large.

Most firms find that door-to-door delivery of cards is the best way to bring in business, though once you are established repeat work will account for a very large proportion. Try to negotiate regular contracts with local hospitals and hotels; if your drivers are self-employed, much of your income as the business owner will come from a percentage of such regular accounts.

You may find it easier to break into this field if you are, for example, an all-woman business dealing only with other women.

Cabinet-making

You need woodworking skill, developed at school or college, and ideally some time spent working with an experienced craftsman. You do not have to invest huge initial sums in tools, though you will need a good workbench, for example; you can certainly operate from a large garage or shed until you are established enough to rent your own workshop. Study magazines such as *Practical Woodworking* for possible secondhand tools, and sources of wood.

Many antique dealers also sell some new furniture in traditional style, and it may be worth seeking out regular commissions here, and building up contacts. Gift and craft shops with, for example, tea-rooms attached, might also make a fruitful market for your work. Most of your sales are likely to come from personal contact, and advertising is probably not going to be worth while.

Cake decorating

There is a substantial market for individually designed cakes for special occasions; to be a success the product must be related to knowledge of the recipient, and look very professional. For this kind of work, you will have to have attend catering college, or at the very least an evening class, and you will have to invest in some basic equipment, such as an ice turntable. But the initial costs are not great: the main problem will be establishing a reputation. It is easy to say that you must build up a word of mouth reputation via your friends, but in the end that is the only way you are likely to make a success of it. You could try local press advertising, but customers are not likely to order unless they have seen some magnificent examples of your work.

Candle-making

This is one form of craftwork with a high fire risk, so make sure your insurance is good. You will need enough room to hang your candles while the wax solidifies; a large garage or shed should be enough to begin with. You may find books helpful; and there may be evening classes in your vicinity.

Like other forms of craft manufacture, the key to success is to aim at the more expensive, quality end of the gift market, and to create your own individual style; there is simply no point in trying to compete with the mass production of the kind of candles used in the event of power failure.

Carpentry

This is one of the traditional building trade skills; you build door and window frames, shelves and cupboards, and of course floorboards. Entry was traditionally by means of apprenticeship, and working for somebody else first is still the only sound way of learning the business. When you do set up on your own, outlay is not too great: tools such as saws and planes, a van and an answering machine. Remember public liability insurance.

Leaflet drops and advertisements in the local press or newsagents' windows are a good idea, but cultivate as many friends as possible in the building industry so that they pass on work to you and you to them. Always give written estimates, and ask for a deposit if you need to spend a lot in advance on materials. As you develop, you can take on an assistant or two, as long as you make sure that the standard of work remains high. There is plenty of demand for this kind of work, and if you stress quality and reliability you should not need to underprice yourself.

Car repairs

Clearly you need a thorough knowledge of cars and car manufacture, and at least two years' experience of garage work; a formal qualification (such as a City and Guilds certificate) could also be useful. Investment is high: you will need to spend a lot of money on basic tools – hydraulic jack, vice, ramp, etc. – and a mobile workshop so that you can work from the client's premises. Forget any idea of working from home; you will never get planning permission. Contact the CAB for detailed legal requirements you must adhere to.

Advertise in local newsagents' windows, and with a leaflet drop, giving examples of costs for typical repairs. Once you are established you should pick up a lot of business through word of mouth. The more contacts you have in the trade, the better; you need to know where you can get parts cheaply and quickly.

Car restoring

As with so many small-business options, there is no point in trying to compete with well-established garages in what they do best, i.e. commonly needed repairs to popular models. The growth in interest in 'classic' cars, which need not be above twenty years old, has created a demand for a much more interesting speciality. You will probably be an enthusiast already and have plenty of friends and acquaintances in the same position; ask them what they pay for the restoration of key instruments and accessories, whether they are satisfied with the quality of work they receive, whether indeed they can find anybody to do the work in the first place.

There are national magazines you could advertise in, at least experimentally, but much of your work is likely to come through personal contact, or through Owners' Clubs and the like. When business starts to take off, you may have difficulty in finding other workers with the necessary enthusiasm and skill. However, one problem you can avoid in this kind of business is that of bad debts, simply by the expedient of not allowing the customer's machine to leave your premises until his or her cheque is cleared; the customer may not like it, and may even be abusive, but you must stick to your guns.

Clearly you are going to need well-secured workshop premises.

Car valet services

The carwash phenomenon is an unsatisfactory one to many proud owners, who none the less lack the time or energy to maintain their vehicles in a pristine state; this is particularly the case in the older, but still wealthier, areas of the larger cities, where there may be few garages in evidence. You could offer a mobile valeting service, charging as much as £25 or more for a really professional steam clean with all the trimmings.

Bold and attractive leaflet drops in carefully targeted areas are the best means of building up business. One disadvantage is that you will probably have to work unsocial hours at weekends and in the evenings when the cars are not in use; however, when you are really in demand you may be able to dictate your own hours to a much greater degree. You could also build up a profitable sideline in carpet cleaning to compensate for periods of rain. There will obviously be some outlay in terms of cleaning equipment, but as with so many personal services of this type the low running costs form one of the major attractions.

Catering for functions

Whatever the economic climate, there will always be weddings, office Christmas parties, private dinner parties, business lunches, and cocktail parties; and there will always be hosts unwilling to cook for even the smallest number of dinner guests and willing to pay professionals handsomely for such a service. It is perfectly possible to be a self-trained cook, but you will probably need some experience in the catering trade, or at least have attended a domestic science course. Be imaginative: try out new ideas (or variants on old ideas) on your family and friends, and, most important, get them to spread the good news around and drum up new business for you. Leave smart business cards wherever you go.

There is a need for some investment at the outset – you must have a large freezer, plenty of sealed containers, and probably also a large oven which you can use exclusively for business. You will need plenty of space (again, preferably a separate part of your home) to store equipment and food in, and of course for the preparation work. You will need reliable transport, and you will need liability insurance against the (hopefully slight) risk of one of the guests going down with food poisoning. For larger fork suppers or wedding receptions, you may be required to supply cutlery, plates and glasses. You will need a partner or employee if you are going to tackle larger functions.

All catering is extremely hard work, very anti-social as far as family life is concerned, and subject to tough legal restrictions: make sure you take advice from the planning and environmental health departments of your local authority, and get copies of the statutory food hygiene regulations from HMSO. Having said all that, it is potentially lucrative, if you can establish a reputation for quality and imagination; charge per head, and always negotiate your fee in advance, when you are deciding what food to prepare. It is probably best to have your own core menu of dishes you do really well, and to vary and extend these as necessary to suit the individual customer. Charges may vary slightly, depending on whether you are asked to serve as well, or simply to melt away so that the hosts can take all the credit for your efforts.

Cat-minding

Too much investment and legal registration is needed to make opening a cattery a good option; in any case, there seems to be a move away from such institutional care and towards the kind of mobile service which is easier to provide, and more satisfactory for all concerned, including the pets. You could advertise your services in newsagents' windows, and try a local leaflet drop; unless you can provide references or word-of-mouth recommendations, you may find owners initially reluctant to entrust you with their house keys, but this sort of problem can be overcome. Some basic veterinary knowledge might be helpful, in case of health problems while the owners are away.

Base your charges on the time you spend in each client's house: if the owner wants you to provide food and cat litter, you can make a profit on these as well. Indeed, you could develop a delivery service for the elderly or housebound. The service need not restrict itself to cats, of course, though dogs are more of a problem because of the need for space and exercise.

Child-minding services

If you are going to run an agency in this field, you will need to include nannying and babysitting within your remit, as wide a range of services as possible, in fact. There is a huge demand among affluent young professionals, who would rather let an agency do the vetting work than have to find their own trustworthy child-minders. You have to be registered as an Employment Agency with the Department of Employment, but otherwise there are no formal qualifications; you will need a desk, a telephone and an answering machine, but you can certainly work from home.

This is a very personal service, and you need to be able to match child-minders to clients as sensitively as possible; obviously the more contacts you have among nannies and registered child-minders looking for work, the better. Local newspapers in affluent areas are a better bet for advertising than the traditional places like *The Lady*.

For supplying full-time nannies, you will want to charge a fee or a percentage of the employee's earnings, to be paid by the client when the nanny starts work; for occasional babysitting you will want to invoice clients periodically – make sure your cash flow can cope with the need to pay the babysitters in the meantime. Obviously the clients will be paying more than they would if they did all the work themselves, but many will be happy to do so, to free more of their own time.

You must be prepared to cope calmly with a crisis in this business, and you must make sure the staff you supply all maintain the highest possible standards; that way you will not only avoid confrontations with angry parents, but be able to acquire a stream of new clients through word-of-mouth recommendation.

China repair

This is highly skilled work, and you must attend courses; you will need a steady hand, excellent eyesight and patience, as well as a natural feel for china. There are two choices of business here: a repair service; or the buying, restoring and selling of china for profit, which is really a branch of antique dealing.

If you are offering a service, you will have to invest several hundred pounds in brushes, paints, glues, and a jeweller's drill, for example, before you can begin. You will need quite a lot of space for the storage of materials, as well as a studio, so you may need to rent a workshop depending on how much space you have at home. What you can earn, and where you can procure business, will both depend very much on how impressive your qualifications are; clearly your aim should be as high as possible, since a dealer will pay a great deal more for the repair of a priceless Chinese vase than your neighbour will for an old teapot. If you can aim high, direct approaches to dealers, topped up perhaps with advertising in trade and collectors' magazines, is the way to advance; in the meantime, the local newsagent may be as good a place to try as any, especially in an affluent area. Customers will need to see evidence of your skills before parting with their valuables, however, and you will need insurance to cover the (no doubt remote) possibility that you destroy the item you should be restoring or if it is stolen from your premises.

Cleaning services

The demand for domestic help services has never been greater, and is likely to increase. Modern families would rather buy in help from an agency than have to deal with an employee. The great advantage of this business is that you do not need any specific qualifications, though obviously it helps if you have worked as a cleaner yourself, even on a casual basis, and are still prepared to get your hands dirty when necessary.

To start an agency, you need transport (for getting your staff from job to job), an answering machine, and imaginative advertising. Try to think of a snappy name for your business, and match that with snappy business cards and leaflets; try to get some free publicity in the local press by making a special introductory offer of a bunch of flowers or similar inducement. Though the market is expanding, the business is a competitive one and you will need to work hard in the early stages to establish yourself.

Students and other young people in need of extra cash may be a good bet to fulfil your staff requirements; get them to work in teams of two so that a house can be cleaned in an hour or two. Pay the staff slightly above normal cleaning rates, to make sure you keep a steady supply of good, reliable workers; make sure you keep all the paperwork up to date and above board. Send your clients regular invoices, and keep an eye on bad debt problems.

Above all, be prepared to offer a variety of services: child-minding as well as cleaning, for example. Clients will pay handsomely if they know they can rely on you to supply all their domestic needs at the drop of a hat; the potential of the domestic service market really does have to be experienced to be believed, but you must have the essential management skills to profit from it.

Clothes hire

There is always a market for clothes hire, especially for weddings and balls, and a big market for fancy dress. The latter is cheaper and easier to break into, if you have the imagination to think up and create some unusual new ideas; the materials will not cost so much, and you do not need to worry so much about stocking every different size. Ideally, you will want a prime High Street site, but this is not essential at the outset; provided that everyone know where to find you and you are reasonably accessible, there is no reason why you should not work from home. You do, however, need a well-lit room with long mirrors and screens. And you will need to invest in a fair-sized stock of the really popular costumes, which you may be able to pick up secondhand.

If you have some interesting and novel ideas in your fancy-dress repertoire, why not try to get the local newspaper interested in a feature article about your business? Otherwise, newspaper advertising could be effective if you have a shop-front, a leaflet drop more useful if you are not so obvious to the passer-by. Ask your party-going friends how much they would pay for hiring a costume, and what sort of costumes they would like to hire; in this way you can keep abreast of party fashions and be prepared.

Colour and interior design advice

A recent trend in interior decoration has been for co-ordination of wallpapers, carpets and fabrics, and you may be able to cash in on this by offering advice to these without the time to decide on their own colour scheme. You will need to be very much aware of the current trends in interior design, visiting trade fairs and making contacts; perhaps the best means of creating a successful business is to negotiate a deal with one or more independent stockists of quality products to take a percentage on the orders received through you. This would, of course, be in addition to the fee you would charge for your services regardless of whether the clients concerned decided to adopt your schemes, a fee worked out on the basis of time spent.

The stockists you deal with would also provide you with samples from which clients could make final choices; you could come to an additional agreement with a local painter and decorator, and offer a complete interior design service. This kind of business will only really develop once you have earned a reputation, but you could try a press release, and a mailshot (with brochure) to the yuppie households in your district.

Computer consultancy

Now that there is a bewildering selection of hardware and software available, many small businesses and individuals will be interested in a truly independent consultant who can decide with them what they need to buy. Your best bet will be to join forces with a small local dealer, through whom you can order stock and take a commission. There is no point in trying to compete on price with the High Street chains; you must emphasize the personal service, your ability to tailor the right system to the particular client, and back-up services you can offer, such as initial training sessions for the company staff.

It goes without saying that you must understand how computers work, but as important is the ability to listen, to understand what the real needs of your clients are and how they can be met within the company price range and in a way which inspires their trust in you. And, of course, you must keep abreast of all the trade developments. If you have taught basic computing skills, for example (which can be combined as a separate part of this business), or have good contacts among local small firms, you may be able to build up a lucrative series of connections fairly quickly. Ask your acquaintances who they buy from, and whether they are satisfied with the service; the answer will almost certainly be no. Mailshots to small businesses are a good idea if you can mention satisfied clients.

Computer programming

Many software houses use freelance computer programmers working from home. These firms may expect you to have your own equipment, or in other cases may provide it. As a first step, you should contact the Association of Independent Computer Specialists, or one of the big firms, such as ICL (International Computers Ltd). Most firms will only consider giving work to those with at least three years' experience in the industry, but freelancers should earn as much as site-based staff.

Computer repairs

Most business computers are maintained through service contracts, but with the enormous growth in sales of home micros, there is a market for repairing and modifying such smaller models. If you have the necessary background of training and work experience within the industry, or have taken a course in computer engineering, it could be worth your while approaching the small independent dealers, who may be prepared to refer business to you from their customers. Advertising locally, or in trade magazines, may also be worth while. Remember to insure yourself against damage you may unwittingly cause to your customers' hardware.

You need a small workshop (or a large garage), a van, and some basic testing equipment, as well as a supply of the most common components.

Conveyancing

As many readers will know, the solicitors' monopoly on conveyancing was ended only in 1985; since then, it has been possible for an individual to be licensed by the Council for Licensed Conveyancers, and after a period of three years working for somebody else, to set up his or her own conveyancing business. Contact the Council, or the Society of Licensed Conveyancers, for more information about the training course and the two-part examination you must pass.

You will need to pay meticulous attention to detail, and be capable of putting worried clients at ease; moving house is a very stressful business. You will make money partly by undercutting local solicitors (check out the competition in your area first), but you can only do that consistently by ensuring that the great bulk of your business is straightforward; you need to develop a nose for the more difficult case which might lead to complications and need the greater legal experience of a solicitor to sort out.

Business can come to you through advertising, but referrals are a better bet; an office above an estate agent's shop is an excellent idea, but make sure you choose an independent agent, rather than a subsidiary of a large financial institution which will prefer to handle its own conveyancing.

Courier/dispatch services

Talk to any business person about the Post Office, and how much frustration is caused by industrial disputes or inefficiency. There are now literally hundreds of independent courier/dispatch firms all over the UK, and competition is likely to remain intense in this expanding market. If you live in or near a major city with a thriving business sector, and have a number of friends or acquaintances who own their own reliable motorcycles and would like to work for you on a self-employed basis, this is not too difficult an operation to set up. There will be some initial investment in radio equipment, which you may rent to your riders, and mailshot or leaflet advertising to firms who are likely to benefit from immediate postal delivery – the advertising and media sectors are always a good bet – but there is certainly no need for plush offices. You must, however, have somebody available to answer the telephone at all times during office hours. Riders will need additional insurance to cover breakages etc, and you may wish to arrange this for them to be safe.

The main problem is going to be to attract and keep riders, which means paying them competitive rates, but at the same time charging clients no more than other firms. Because the competition is already so intense, price is not a major factor in attracting new business: speed and reliability are much more crucial. You may do better to start off with same-day deliveries of small packets and letters, and perhaps to improve speed by concentrating on smaller areas – the City of London, or the M4 high-tech corridor would be examples. There are even dispatch cyclists and walkers, who mainly patrol the short distances between foreign embassies and government buildings in the Belgravia district of London.

Crèche provision

Perhaps you discover that local firms are experiencing problems in recruiting full-time staff because potential applicants have children at home; if you have experience in child-care, you could telephone the managing directors of such firms, suggesting that they might like to offer crèche facilities as an employment inducement, and that you are in a position to manage such facilities.

Contact the local Social Services Department for advice on the laws governing crèches (all private day care provision must be registered with the local authority, for example), and for information on which facilities already exist in the area. If you can find similar firms which have already benefited from setting up such services for their employees, so much the better. Of course, there is nothing to stop you setting up a business for private individuals, but if you can negotiate a number of separate deals with local firms, you may be in a position to make a great deal more money, and indeed to perform an overall managerial role rather than engaging in the child-care aspects personally. Whether this is an advantage depends on whether the biggest appeal lies in the money-making potential or in the opportunities to surround yourself with children. Charges will have to be based on the number of children and employees involved. The potential for a thriving business may be limited only by the difficulty in attracting suitable staff.

Disc jockey

Obviously you must enjoy working at night, and you will need to have a strong outgoing personality and be at ease with all sorts of people. There is a considerable initial investment needed here – an amplifier, speakers, microphones, mixers, and an exciting light show are all prerequisites, quite apart from a record collection.

You will need to be very much aware of your local competitors, how much they charge, and what they offer. Get yourself invited to plenty of local discos and see how you could improve on what is available. You need the 'unique selling proposition'; ask around and find out what people like and what they hate. Then put together an exciting mailshot and sell yourself to local firms, schools and colleges, societies, hotels and restaurants. Aim to be the best in the neighbourhood, and you will have no problem in commanding a higher fee. But you must always keep abreast of changing trends and never become stale.

Dressmaking

Many of the points connected with knitwear also apply here: you have a choice of selling your services to manufacturers, or marketing your own products through shops or even directly (via mail order) to members of the public. It is best to specialize: in maternity wear, baby wear, large sizes, wedding gowns. Any clothes made professionally must always look just that – very professional; each garment must be labelled with its size and country of origin, and washing instructions are also obligatory. In any clothes-related business, a snappy name is an asset, especially if you are dealing directly with the public. As always, too, it is that elusive individual quality which is most sought. Read *DR: The Fashion Business* to assess market trends, and find your own gap.

Driving instruction

First contact the Driving Instructors' Association to obtain details of how to take the Department of Transport examination (both written and practical) to become an approved instructor; professional training is not cheap, but it is essential. You must have had a full clean licence for at least four years. When you qualify, you should of course also have at least one saloon car, appropriately fitted with L-plates and with dual control. You can happily work from home with an answering machine, and initial investment in advertising should not need to be very great: perhaps a short run in the local newspaper, reinforced with a leaflet drop, and all emphasizing a special introductory offer of the 'two lessons for the price of one' kind.

Learning to drive is a highly stressful experience; you need to be a sympathetic teacher, good at calming nerves and capable of building confidence when required. If you can accomplish this, and have the knack of achieving a high pass rate by entering each pupil for his or her test only when the optimum time arrives, you should build a strong reputation by word of mouth. In time, you can take on other instructors on a self-employed basis, but good instructors are often difficult to attract and keep unless you pay top rates and take less of a cut yourself. You will have to do as much teaching as possible in the evenings and at weekends. And you must have sufficient capital available to be able to replace your cars every year or two; they will need it.

Egg decoration

Decorated eggs of different sizes look particularly beautiful on a well-arranged stall at a craft market, and the larger goose eggs can sell for as much as £20; whether this is economic depends on how fast you can work, as well as the cost of materials, such as the satin you may want to line the larger eggs with, so that they can be opened up to be used to store jewellery.

There is increasing interest in this craft, and there may be an adult education class in your area. You practise on a blown hen's egg, and move on to the more exotic varieties later. It is also possible to decorate eggs made of pottery, wood, china or glass but the delicacy of the true egg is what attracts most people. You must find your own individual designs, as well as taking special orders, and what you charge will vary greatly, depending partly on your skill, but mainly on where you are selling. So aim for a quality craft market in an area that is likely to attract many visitors.

Electrical work

A traditional kind of self-employment. Few DIY enthusiasts are prepared to tackle large electrical jobs, and there is an increasing awareness of cowboys, so there should be plenty of work here for somebody with qualifications. You can train with your local Electricity Board, or by working for another electrician and attending a college course to gain the City and Guilds certificate. References from satisfied customers will be your most valuable advertisement. Advertisements in the Yellow Pages and local newspapers are useful, and you could try a leaflet drop. The aim should always be to obtain as many larger jobs – from house rewires upwards to institutional work – as possible. Find out how much the competition is charging by inviting estimates on your (or a friend's) house, but do not be tempted to undercut: there is plenty of work, and customers are willing to pay handsomely for skilled labour and peace of mind. Play on this by offering a guarantee. Enrol with the National Inspection Council for Electrical Installation Contracting, and use the fact in your advertising.

Start-up costs in this business are not great, though you will need some specialized tools, and a van. However, the materials you buy for each job are expensive, so you will need to obtain at least a proportion of your charges upfront, unless the customer is known to you, and your trust in him or her is total: once you have installed a new electrical system, you cannot very easily rip out your handiwork in protest against non-payment. This kind of business can soon develop so that you need to take on extra skilled labour, in which case cash flow and credit control become even more important.

Employment agency

Think of setting up an employment agency only if you intend to specialize in a particular field of work – accountancy, law, computing – and have a good deal of experience and many contacts among both firms and staff in that line of business. This is because big firms with well-known names are so well established in the broader recruitment field that they will inevitably attract most firms and staff, making it difficult for a newcomer to get established.

You will need a licence from the Department of Employment, and to comply with the Employment Agencies Act; this means maintaining very detailed records, so make sure you study the Department's booklet on the Act before you start trading.

Do not deal in temporary staff, at least to begin with – the capital requirements will be too great, since the staff will expect you to pay them weekly, while your clients pay you monthly. If, on the other hand, you charge your clients 10 or 15 per cent of the annual salary on each permanent placement, and you take that money in advance (when the newcomer starts work), your cash-flow position is an advantageous one. This sounds good, in the sense that you do not have to make many sales to make a profit, but remember that ten interviews or more may be necessary before you find the right person for the right job. This is very much a selling business: selling one of the staff on your books to a firm who has a need. Indeed, it is quite possible to see who is advertising for your kind of staff, and ring the firms concerned a few days later to find out whether they are suited or not. But remember, if you send firms unsatisfactory employees, they will never come back again.

You do not have to have plush street-window premises; space in a modern business centre might be better. But do advertise in appropriate local and specialist media to make sure that staff know where to find you. As with all agency work, the problem is to attract a steady stream of high-calibre staff for you to place.

One variation is to specialize in, say, the building industry, where large firms often have a short-term need for a gang of five labourers and a carpenter, or whatever. If you know a lot of people who do this kind of work on a self-employed or casual basis, you could supply the labour, handling all the paperwork, and taking a nice profit either by charging the large firm, or by taking a percentage of the employee's earnings, or both. But you do need lots of contacts to call on.

Enamelling

This is a typical form of craftwork, probably involving a local college course at the outset. You will need lots of space in which to keep your tools and your kiln; you must be aware of the fire risk, and make sure you have adequate insurance. There are plenty of books available, and good craft shops from which you may be able to purchase raw materials in bulk, and later use to sell your products.

As with all such products, you must have a natural design flair and an ability to create your own distinctive style. If so, and if there is a demand for your products, you can set your prices high.

Estate agency

The position may change in the future, but under the 1979 Estate Agents Act, it is fair to say that almost anybody can become an estate agent, though there are certain rules which must be followed concerning the handling of money and the keeping of records. However, if you are attracted by the apparently lucrative nature of this business, and you think you are good at selling, do get some experience working for somebody else first. There is usually work available somewhere; most firms pay a small basic salary topped up with commission, so if you are really good you may find you make so much money that much of the urge towards self-employment is removed.

Any fool can sell houses in a boom period, and you may think that the established agents in your area are all charging far too much, and want to undercut them accordingly. But if you do that, will you still be making enough money to cover your overheads and survive when the market is far more depressed? Your 'unique selling proposition' is going to have to be based on more than just a lower commission figure. Look at the structure of estate agency in your area: is most of the business done by the huge financial chains, as is certainly the case in most places now? If so, there may be a market for a more personal service, based perhaps on a more lavish brochure style of presentation, a slightly but significantly lower commission, and an emphasis on the uniqueness of each property and independence from financial interests. Choose your area very carefully, and make sure you can afford to rent a shopfront in a prime High Street site.

This is a business ideal for two partners; you are always going to need one person to cover the office when the other is out valuing properties or showing potential purchasers around. Many estate agents make a high proportion of their income from arranging mortgages and insurance for their clients, but if you want to do this you will need to be registered under the Financial Services Act; it may be better to retain somebody to do this for you on a part-time basis, at least in the early stages.

Events organizing

This is likely to mean setting up promotional events for corporate clients, but could mean, for example, organizing weddings for private individuals. The idea is that the client leaves you to supply everything from the venue and the food to the entertainment, while giving the impression to guests that everything has been done in-house.

Set-up costs are not great – you must have an answering machine and other office equipment like a photocopier and word processor – but the key to this business is making contacts with reliable suppliers of everything your clients are going to want to have supplied. You must be very well organized with an outgoing personality; a background in public relations could be useful. Besides your own fees, charged on an hourly basis, you will charge commission on the products and services you supply, but you will of course have to pay for these while waiting for your client to pay you. Because of this, you must get a deposit from the client, and keep a careful check on your cash flow.

Always make sure at the outset that what the client wants can be done within the budget; that way you prevent any misunderstandings and accusations of bad faith later on. Almost all business is likely to come through personal contact, and in theory at least each major job well done ought to lead to another. There may be scope for some free journal publicity.

Exhibition design

If you have a design qualification, and perhaps some industrial or retail contacts, this might be a good area to think about, since few smaller firms tend to employ exhibition designers full-time. The work involves planning the flow of an exhibition, and making sure that fire and safety regulations are adhered to, as well as arranging the appearance of the actual displays.

You need somewhere to work, but that can be at home, and aside from some design equipment, costs are not too great. The contacts are the thing – once you have two or three successful design projects to your credit, approaches to potential new clients will be much more fruitful.

Fashion consultancy

Advising business people in particular on their choice of clothes, and on co-ordinating clothes and accessories to achieve an overall impact, is a small but expanding market. You may find a background in beauty consultancy helpful, and you will need to know how executives can complement natural colour with clothes, the technique of colour analysis. There are courses available, though these are more prevalent in the US than in Britain; organizations such as the London College of Fashion may be able to provide information or contact addresses. Or work for one of the existing companies in the field.

There is no substitute for media publicity in this kind of business; any coverage you can obtain on local radio or TV, or in local newspapers, will be valuable. You will need to rent space, and you could do worse than see whether any prominent beauty salon in your neighbourhood has a spare room available.

Initially, you may want to charge individual clients by the hour. As you become better known, you could mailshot local businesses and professional organizations and offer courses to senior staff, for one large and all-inclusive fee. At the outset, you may encounter resistance from the traditionally minded (such as bank managers); you will have to sell yourself, to convince them that the technique is scientifically valid, and that you have the knowledge and experience to use it effectively. This is not as simple as it sounds, particularly as the colour analysis world is itself divided between the cruder 'seasonal' approach which seeks to categorize each person as a spring, summer, autumn or winter type, and a more sophisticated emphasis on the unique colouring of each individual.

Frozen meals

Another variation on the catering theme. You will need a lot of freezer space, so it may be worth looking at the possibility of buying secondhand commercial freezers; when you draw up your business plan, remember to include the annual running costs as well as the initial capital expenditure.

Pubs are likely to represent your major potential market; ring them up first, send them smartly printed menus, and then visit them with one or two samples of your wares. The main principles are to keep your range of meals fairly small, changing them from time to time; use fresh ingredients wherever possible; and provide really big helpings – that is what the customers are going to want. Avoid the temptation to be too experimental, at least until you are really well established.

If you are selling in reasonable bulk in advance, you will have to make your prices attractive enough for the pubs to be able to afford the outlay; however, the great advantage over most other types of catering business is that because you are not responsible for actually selling the product to the public, you are not left with any waste and you can therefore calculate your profit margins much more precisely.

Gardening

This is rather like window-cleaning: a traditional mainstay of the self-employed, a service which more and more busy people want and complain about not being able to find. This should, in theory, mean that you ought to be able to increase your charges, in more affluent areas at least.

The great advantage gardening has over window-cleaning is that only a few regular clients are needed for a full-time job to be created; local newsagents' windows are the best place to begin advertising, unless you feel confident enough to send a mailshot to specific wealthy individuals whose gardens look as if they need some work done on them.

Of course, the big drawback is always going to be the British climate, unless your clients have extensive greenhouses and work to keep you occupied when it rains and snows. Most people are primarily going to be interested in lawn-mowing and weeding, but you may be able to command higher rates if you can suggest ways of improving or even redesigning the plot of land. Hint that you are much in demand; if you can provide references, so much the better.

Garden design

Think not so much of laying out acres of parkland in the manner of Capability Brown, but of a much more intimate concept. You might have a background in botany or horticulture, or in a design discipline, or even in technical drawing, or you might simply be a knowledgeable gardener with creative flair. If you are going to earn a lot of money, you will need formal training, possibly on a government training scheme; ask at your local Jobcentre for availability and contact the

Institute of Horticulture or the Landscape Institute, which publishes a journal, *Landscape Design*.

At the top end of the scale, you can earn huge sums for laying out the gardens of millionaires' mansions, but in the early stages you will need to establish a reputation locally. You could try a mailshot, expensively produced to emphasize that you are not just a jobbing gardener, and perhaps offering a free initial consultation to explain your services more effectively. Besides your own fee, you can take a profit on materials or shrubs you order for your client. You do not need a separate office, but an answering machine is a must. And, of course, you will need to invest a fair amount in really good tools. As soon as you are established, you will want to think about employing an assistant to cover the heavy labouring jobs, leaving you more time to devote to the creative side. Not an easy business to break into, but immensely satisfying and rewarding for the successful.

Glazing

You will need a special van for carrying glass and cutting tools, but start-up costs are not great. Work for a glazing firm, or do a course for a City and Guilds certificate, and make sure you are adequately insured.

There is always work available if you are prepared to offer a 24-hour service fitting broken shop windows, for example. Or you can work for small builders on a self-employed basis, fitting windows to new houses, or deal in more specialized fields such as double-glazing, though here you may find it difficult to compete with the big firms and their advertising budgets.

You should obtain a good deal of business through contacts in the building trade; otherwise try leaflet drops, and local advertising.

Graphic design

You must have studied graphic design, and aim to specialize in publishing, for example, or advertising. Essentially you are creating images for companies, interpreting what they want, doing a rough draft and amending it in discussion, and then perhaps commissioning an artist to produce a final version of your design.

You need very little in the way of equipment, but you do need as many contacts as possible; business is likely to come in this way, though you may wish to advertise your services in marketing journals, or try a direct approach to a few firms. It might be worth contacting the Design Council to see if it would be prepared to recommend you.

Graphology

Graphology is the analysis of character through handwriting, and is increasingly used by management in large organizations to help in the recruitment of staff; there are now a number of introductory books available. Training is not easy, unless you can find another graphologist prepared to take you on; try the Graphology Centre for possible options. You can of course work from home, so start-up costs are minimal.

Though you can advertise for private clients, it is a much better idea to approach firms in your area directly, particularly medium-sized firms who may not yet have taken on board this relatively new technique. You will need to spend a lot of time in the early stages convincing potential clients of your worth, so an attractive explanatory brochure will help, especially if you can include testimonials. Charge by the hour, depending on your experience.

You need to have a good knowledge of human psychology to do this job well; the two areas are by no means in conflict, as is often supposed.

Hairdressing

There is no shortage of potential hairdressing businesses, and those who want to follow this well-travelled route will of course have been apprenticed and trained. There is a big potential market for travelling hairdressers, especially among older people, and this is the obvious choice for somebody with limited capital: you will need a reliable car, an answering machine to pick up bookings, and your own essential equipment. Cost your service carefully, avoiding the temptation to charge too little; advertise through local newsagents, local newspapers, leaflet drops, and word of mouth; you should pick up enough regular clients to earn a living, as long as this kind of service is not already being offered extensively in your locality. Another option is to come to an arrangement with a local hotel and pay commission from your earnings.

Opening your own salon is much more difficult, and it is almost essential to have gained management experience with another operation to be able to demonstrate a track record of business efficiency and profitability; a bank is not going to lend you money without this. There are also a number of franchise possibilities in this field, but again capital requirements will be considerable.

Because hairdressing is such an obvious service, there is always a danger of saturation; do your market research thoroughly.

Health foods

All the signs are that this retail market will grow and grow in the years ahead. But there are really two kinds of business you can run here. The more lucrative financially will involve the wholesale as well as the retail side: that means selling bulk quantities of foods to shops and restaurants. If you are to move into this kind of business, you need to make sure that there is a real need for the service in your area, and that you have reliable and suitable transport; the location of your premises will not be so important because you will not be relying on passing trade to earn a living.

Retail businesses tend to sell homoeopathic remedies as much as food, and may also branch into bookselling and support for local community groups. This could be very rewarding, and there is plenty of scope for you to become a leading figure in the local community, but the rewards are less likely to be so strong financially.

In either case, the usual hygiene regulations connected with any food selling apply; advance market research into the needs of a particular community are even more important in this field than for most other businesses. In any case, you are unlikely to be interested unless you already have good contacts among suppliers and customers.

House history

Much the same qualifications are needed as for ancestry research; indeed, the two businesses could be combined, since the people who lived in a house are as interesting as the bricks and mortar, and records you use tend to overlap. A basic knowledge of architecture and interior decoration is useful to enable you to spot fakes and alterations. *Tracing the History of Your House* by Peter Bushell (Pavilion Books), is a recent, though rather simple, introduction to the subject; *Sources for the History of Houses* by J. H. Harvey (British Records Association) is more advanced.

Those expensive magazines you are always looking at and never buying – *Traditional Homes, Homes and Gardens, Country Living* – are a good bet for an advertising launch. If you have a special knowledge of or interest in a particular town or district, you could try a direct mailshot (get the names of current owners from the electoral register at the library). Again, if you know an area really well, make friends with the local estate agents, who are always looking for ways to make houses sound really special; they might commission you on a regular basis to write short histories for their brochures. And again, get plenty of press releases and interesting news stories. But in all this, do make sure you are working in an upmarket area, where the householders really have the money to spend on such inessentials.

Travel costs and perhaps advertising are the most significant expenses. You will probably want to charge an hourly rate based on your knowledge and experience, though if you do business with estate agents they may prefer an all-inclusive fee; if this happens you must be prepared to keep track of your time very carefully to ensure you are sticking to your margins.

Import/export

Essentially all you are doing here is introducing potential suppliers and purchasers, deciding on price and taking a commission. There are no special qualifications needed, and you do not have to be licensed, but you do need contacts in particular industries or countries. Contacts are what this business is all about.

Start with a product you know to be in demand, and a potential buyer, and find a supplier, rather than the other way round. Since your commission will be on a percentage basis, you can afford to keep it low if you are dealing in large quantities. When you start, you will need to put up some initial capital to buy from suppliers (though the bulk of the cost will be provided by banks); once you start receiving income, things will be much easier. There is not a great deal of risk involved, as long as you make sure you can sell everything you buy, that your supplier has any necessary permits, and that your finance and insurance are reputably arranged and properly documented. The British Overseas Trade Board will fill you in on VAT and customs regulations, though they will obviously be more keen to help you if you are involved in exporting British goods overseas.

This kind of business is ideal for the older person with good contacts in industry; set-up costs are minimal, though you must be able to telex/ fax information, and a London address might inspire confidence.

Industrial design

You will need to have substantial work experience as a design engineer in industry. Your market will be smaller companies, too small to employ full-time designers of their own. Put together an attractive business card, letterhead and brochure, with a strong company logo – remember it is design ability you are selling. Make a list of local firms who might be interested in your services, and the name of the relevant manager or chief engineer within each one; telephone them all and outline what you can offer. Only a small proportion will be interested – perhaps one in eight – but subsequent meetings should enable you to build up a small base of regular client firms from which you can develop.

As you expand you may need to take on extra specialist staff, such as a draughtsperson, and short-term contract labour for particularly heavy jobs. As with any such freelance consultancy work, your fees will be difficult to judge initially, but may have to be based around what a full-time designer would command.

Jewellery making

As with any such craft item, individuality and an instantly recognizable style are a must. There are plenty of courses available, and many different materials can be used. It will certainly be worth subscribing to the *Retail Jeweller* (the jewellers' trade magazine), via which you may be able to obtain materials in bulk and more cheaply.

You can try selling your wares from market stalls, preferably in top tourist locations, or to independently owned boutiques; the more outlets you have the better.

Knitting and crochet

It is possible to write directly to manufacturers or designers, who will then ask you to send in a sample garment made in their own wool and using a variety of stitches: names can be selected from the *Branded Textile Merchandise and Trade Marks Directory*. But you will make more money by approaching local shops; baby and maternity wear specialists are the most likely to buy, but expensive independent boutiques are what you should aim for. Good regular connections with a number of customers are essential, and you will have to invest in a knitting machine.

You will find the *DR: The Fashion Business* useful for leads on where to buy materials. If you can follow fashion trends carefully, and pilot your own designs, you can achieve the highest earnings. In general, the thinner the wool and the more intricate the pattern, the higher the earnings. You may be able to get advice from the Wool Secretariat. If you are aiming for the top, there is simply no point in competing with the machine knitting market – go for more expensive handmade garments, with bright colours and exotic patterns. The British Handknitting Association will supply names and addresses of yarn manufacturers.

Lampshade making

You will need some sewing ability, and there are plenty of courses and books available to help you. Basic equipment is not expensive, but you will need to buy silks and exotic materials to stretch over wire frames; the market for your work will not be good unless your products are outstanding and unusual enough for you to interest the specialist lighting shops. Make sure you are aware of safety standards.

You could try selling directly to the public, either by leaflet drop or door-to-door calls on newcomers, but you are likely to have much more success on your own market stall, or selling through shops. With experience you can make as many as ten lampshades per day, so if you can command high prices for a high-quality product, you can make a very good living doing this.

Leatherwork

There are plenty of courses available, and tools are not too expensive, though you will have to invest in a heavy-duty sewing machine, and a machine for trimming edges; try *Shoe and Leather News* for possible secondhand bargains. It is quite impossible to compete with cheap imports; the high price of leather even when bought wholesale from a tannery means that you must charge high prices to cover your expenses, and therefore that your work must be of a very high quality and originality to sell. Look at prices in galleries and specialist shops to see how much the market will stand.

This is not something you can afford to go into without some detailed market research, so contact potential buyers with samples of your handbags, wallets or belts before you begin to trade seriously. You might also try a market stall or two, though customers are less inclined to buy larger items in such circumstances. There is also a market for bespoke saddles, made to fit a particular horse, so it could be worth contacting riding schools.

Light removals

You must have a reliable secondhand van, and an answering machine, and you need to be based in an urban area. Since many items will be too heavy for one person to lift, it is an advantage to have a partner, or alternatively a pool of friends and acquaintances prepared to be hired casually for a day or two's work. With all this cash floating around, you are obviously going to have to be careful about keeping accounts.

You can advertise in local newspapers, in newsagents' windows, or by leaflet drop, but a better way to generate regular business is by making contact with local auction rooms, furniture stores and garden centres, offering your services for those of their customers who buy items too large to fit into their cars. This kind of business can also be combined with courier and/or minicab work. Give a business card to anybody you have dealings with.

Even more lucrative is to build up relationships with a group of small firms who can give you regular work distributing their products.

Mailing list broking

The direct mail industry is growing rapidly in this country, and the broker is a key component. Rather than maintaining huge numbers of lists yourself, your job is to locate the lists your customers want, and take a commission, perhaps as much as 20 per cent on the rental fee charged by the companies which own the lists. Because there are now so many lists available, brokers tend to specialize in particular fields. The most lucrative lists are those based on in-depth market research, rather than the ones which are simply names and addresses of local professionals from directories.

A background in direct marketing is essential; you must know the kind of information customers are likely to want, where it may be available, how much they can expect to pay for it. The more contacts you have in your chosen areas of interest, the better. Start-up costs are not high, though this is one area where a computer and a good database will be a worthwhile investment. Make sure you know all about the Data Protection Act. The British List Brokers' Association is a regulatory body worth contacting.

Management consultancy

This field has boomed in the business climate of recent years and with the increased emphasis on efficiency and cost-consciousness. You need a strong record of employment and achievement in a management field, such as personnel, and preferably lots of contacts; you must also be an excellent report writer. It would be helpful to be in touch with a group of specialists in different disciplines, who might be prepared to work for you on a freelance basis whenever their expertise was required.

Impressive presentational literature is essential, and you must be prepared to telephone chief executives of smaller companies and persuade them that your services are a necessity and not an expensive luxury. Most consultants charge a daily fee, which can be hundreds of pounds for one individual's advice, the idea being that the fee will none the less be recovered by the client in the savings resulting from improved systems. This sounds attractive, but it is liable to become an increasingly competitive market, and only those with the combination of real management know-how and self-selling ability are likely to survive and thrive.

Market gardening

Research is essential here: you must visit garden centres before you start to trade, or even to plant, and establish precisely what and how much they will buy. In general, there is less competition to grow and sell the more exotic vegetables, flowers and herbs, so it could be a good idea to concentrate on such varieties.

The horticultural section of the National Farmers' Union should be able to give you some general advice.

Market trading

The great advantages of a market stall are that it is cheap, and it is flexible – you can work as many days as you like, and if something fails to sell, you can sell something else next week. There are two vital principles to bear in mind: get a good site in a busy market, even if you have to wait for it to become available; and look at what other traders are selling, so that you can spot the gaps in the market. If you are thinking of trading on a local authority patch, you will need to apply for either a permanent or a casual licence; you can either rent your stall or build your own; and you will need a van to store and transport stock.

This kind of market research is important, because you will want to buy in bulk so as to qualify for a discount from the wholesalers. Study *Trader* to see what is being advertised and for how much, and you will begin to see what is value for money. You will also find that other traders are extremely helpful, as long as you are not selling the same type of stock. This is important because you will want somebody else to mind your stall while you have a tea break.

Marriage bureau

This is perhaps a somewhat old-fashioned term for what many would think of as a dating agency, but in practice marriage is still the ultimate aim for most potential clients of such services. There is clearly no point in trying to compete with the national, or even international, high-technology approach of the big computer dating agencies with their huge advertising budgets. Your aim must be to provide a more specialized (whether by locale, age range, kind of occupation, or whatever) and more personal service. You will need a sympathetic personality; some experience of agency work, marriage guidance or interviewing would be an asset.

You should aim for a suite of offices, to include a comfortable sitting-room where clients can be interviewed and, where appropriate, introduced. You will also have to spend a good deal on advertising, probably in local newspapers to begin with. Choose an affluent area – professionals are the most consistent buyers of this kind of service. Give some thought to the name of the business and the presentation of your sales literature; both must reflect the image you want to put across. The usual system is to charge an initial registration fee and then a further fee for a set period of six months or a year, during which a minimum number of introductions are guaranteed; contact as many other such firms as you can to find out what questions they ask potential clients, and what they offer.

Such businesses are usually run by women, but there is no earthly reason why a man (or indeed a husband and wife team) should not be as effective. You may find it helpful to contact and join the Association of British Introduction Agencies.

Model making

If you have a knowledge of architecture and contacts in the profession, you may be able to make models for such firms. Besides architects themselves, you might approach planning authorities, building societies and other small businesses using display items from time to time. Keep your eyes open; this is such a specialized field that you can command high prices, and you only need a relatively small number of regular business or professional clients to earn a good living.

Mushroom farming

You need specialist knowledge, so join the Mushroom Growers' Association (a branch of the NFU), and study the journal and the other reading matter recommended.

You cannot operate commercially from a garage or a small patch of garden; you need the equivalent of a smallholding or small factory unit. One such successful business occupies damp premises underneath railway arches in central London, which should give you the general idea of what is required. You will need planning permission for a mushroom farm.

If you produce enough of your product, you can sell to wholesalers, and have a virtually guaranteed regular income.

Musical instrument repairs

It is usual to specialize in, for example, wind or string instruments; there is a range of courses offered by such colleges as the London College of Furniture which may be worth investigating. Try to gain some work experience with an instrument manufacturer, and make as many contacts as you can among professional musicians and among students at local music colleges and schools. Distribute business cards giving details of your specialities.

You do not need a great deal of space, so you can work from home, but you will need to invest in the best possible drills and other equipment. Charge on the basis of your time plus the cost of materials. You can advertise in journals such as *The Musician*, but direct contact is more likely to be effective; you might also develop sidelines: selling instruments you have restored, or selling accessories such as reeds for wind instruments.

Newsletter publishing

Perhaps you are a parent of young children and you know there is a real need for a regular magazine or newsletter containing information about local facilities for children and their parents: which pubs welcome families; what are local nursery schools like; where can you find an entertainer for a party? You will need to decide how often to publish (two or three times a year may be enough), how many copies you will be able to distribute (perhaps by totting up membership numbers for relevant local organizations), and hence what it is going to cost you to print and how much advertising space you need to sell to local businesses to make a profit. It is almost certainly going to be easier to work on the basis of free distribution, at least in your first publishing venture.

Selling advertising space should not be too difficult, provided that you have a clear idea of your market and can show evidence that you are capable of reaching the numbers you say you can. Advertisers will be much happier to advertise if you are reaching one of their target markets. You must have good relations with the local groups associated with your target market – for example, playgroups, primary school PTAs, and the National Childbirth Trust, as well as libraries and even tourist centres. The point is that the principle could be applied to any other large local market – teenagers, pensioners, perhaps even recent arrivals from another part of the country if you live in a boom district.

A more sophisticated variant would be the specialized newsletter directed at affluent interest groups prepared to pay handsomely for detailed and up-to-date information: expatriates might be one example. Here you produce the newsletter on a more frequent basis, charging a high (though often tax-deductible) subscription. The possibilities are almost limitless if you really have the knowledge and contacts in your chosen field to generate the steady flow of hard information required. You can buy a mailing list of potential subscribers from a broker, and send out a sample issue to each person; if subscriptions are paid annually in advance, you should not have cash-flow worries. Profits are good, because the newsletter need only be cheaply printed; readers are paying for information, not presentation.

Office administration

If you skipped the administrative sections of this book because you worked for years as a general manager or office manager, this one could be for you. You might think that no companies would want such cover, but do not forget the holiday season, when losing key personnel for weeks on end can plunge any firm into chaos. Maternity leave is another obvious cause of such disruption. Many small and medium-sized firms rely very much on one or two staff to run the details and systems, leaving the directors or partners free to generate new business or perform whatever services they provide for their clients. If you are really professional, you can fill the gap in a way that a standard temporary secretary cannot.

Personal contacts are vital in this kind of business; if people are going to entrust their companies to you, it is imperative that you are totally reliable and dependable. If you can get a couple of short-term assignments from prominent local firms, that will help enormously when you approach others in the area. Again, direct mail, following up with telephone calls, is the way to make the initial contact. As you become better known and in demand, you can both increase your fees and take on staff of your own to become an agency; however, you will have to vet any employees very carefully to ensure that none lets down the reputation you have so carefully built up.

Keep a low profile: remember your job is to keep things moving, not to criticize existing systems. Remember too you may face jealousy from permanent staff, and you will be judged by your results. Be as effective and productive as you can be, friendly but busy.

Organic farming

An increasing number of people want to eat food that has been grown without the use of chemical fertilizers or pesticides. Because of that, there is a great deal of potential in an organic farming business, but it is potential that cannot be realized overnight; do not even think about this business if you are looking for quick profits. Obviously you are not going to be able to start off by buying huge tracts of land; start with what you have and concentrate in the initial stages on learning how to manage weed and pest control without chemicals; there is no substitute for experience.

Support networks are now fairly well organized, and you should be able to obtain help and advice from the Soil Association and its affiliates and, on the finance and marketing sides, from the Rural Development Commission. 'Organic systems require a high level of management to maximize returns, including marketing', says the RDC; you have to avoid the temptation to compete on price, and insist on a premium. The rewards are perhaps not primarily financial; you need to be committed to the product.

Painting and decorating

On the one hand, the DIY boom has meant that you have to offer a higher level of professional skill to make a living from painting and decorating; on the other, we are still talking about a personal service which the more affluent are very happy to pay for, given that level of skill. Doing a local course could be invaluable in teaching you some of the tricks of the trade.

You can advertise in newsagents' windows, or with a leaflet drop to a well-heeled area, but most of your business is bound to come from personal recommendation, and in the early stages testimonials from satisfied customers could be invaluable. Remember that many customers will be leaving you on your own in their houses, so a high degree of trust is implied.

Be prepared to quote for each job individually in advance, avoiding the temptation to sell yourself short; you can also take a small profit on the cost of materials such as paint and wallpaper which you buy on the customer's behalf. Capital outlay is very low, but make sure you have really good-quality brushes to look every inch the skilled professional, and plenty of dustsheets. There is a British Decorators' Association, and many painters are members of the Federation of Master Builders or the Guild of Master Craftsmen, especially if they combine decorating skills with the ability to take on other smaller building jobs.

Photography

This is not an easy market to break into – you will have to specialize and concentrate on building a reputation. It is possible to make a living from concentrating on weddings and family portraits, but there is always going to be a good deal of competition here. A better idea might be a mailshot to local small businesses who may be putting together publicity material and need good photographs of their products and/or premises. Follow up such letters with telephone calls, and make sure you have a strong portfolio to impress potential clients with; it could open up the prospect of regular work. If you have no formal training, the British Institute of Professional Photographers will provide details of approved courses.

An alternative is to go through a more specialist training course, join the Institute of Incorporated Photographers, and concentrate on selling news photographs to periodicals. The chief disadvantage here is that you are limited to a fixed scale of charges; the chief advantage is that you may be given access to accident scenes, for example, by virtue of your credentials.

There is a fair amount of capital outlay – apart from good cameras, you will need processing equipment, and a well-equipped studio and darkroom, possibly at home.

Piano tuning

Apart from having a really good ear for music, it is essential to have worked for another tuner. Most tuners tend to offer restoration and repair work as well as tuning proper, and if this is your aim you may want to contact the London College of Furniture to find out about available courses. There is some initial expenditure on tools, and you will need a garage or workshop if you intend to take instruments away, but start-up costs are very reasonable.

There is certainly a market for a local, door-to-door piano tuner – try cards in newsagents' windows, or some local press advertising – but you are unlikely to make a very good living from this alone. A much better approach is direct contact with local piano teachers, schools and colleges, recording studios and concert halls. Any instrument which is being used by professionals is going to require more frequent attention, simply because perfect tuning is essential to use.

Smart business cards and stationery are never wasted, but personal trust is most important.

Picture framing

There is a lot of High Street competition, often within the franchise format; you must stop thinking of the traditional craftsman taking a fortnight over each job, and learn something from those High Street outlets. You will find that a combination of the best possible equipment and organization of the workshop into a few simple stages, allowing a constant throughput of work, will both contribute to a much more cost-effective business. That said, you will have to be prepared to invest a good deal of initial capital in that equipment, as well as on courses which may be available locally. If you can work for someone else for a while and see the business from the inside, so much the better.

Rather than taking a High Street shopfront yourself, why not emphasize a personal, quality approach, so that the customer sees you as the kind of person they can entrust their prized watercolours to? Aim for the top end of the market with a well-produced brochure explaining the craftsmanship involved, which you can leave with art galleries or photographic shops; advertise in local newspapers, as long as your locality is affluent enough, and try for some feature publicity; do not be afraid to charge more than the franchises; offer a free collection and delivery service; sell prints and posters, framed or unframed. With that kind of approach, you may be able to carve a niche for yourself in what is at first glance a competitive field.

Plumbing

Cowboys are particularly rife in this business, or at least they appear to be to most householders faced with burst pipes in times of cold weather; how many of the cowboys stay in plumbing when the weather turns fine and the pickings are less glaringly obvious is not known. The genuine plumber might do well to resist the temptation to overcharge for that burst pipe, and instead to concentrate on building up a series of strong personal recommendations for honesty and quality, which should aid the development of a much more secure all-year-round business.

Trade associations are important in maintaining standards among skilled traders, and membership of such an association is also a valuable selling tool to be emblazoned on business cards and in the Yellow Pages or local newspapers. You should certainly contact the Institute of Plumbing to find out how to train and become registered, and the Federation of Master Builders or the Guild of Master Craftsmen may also be helpful.

You will have to invest in some tools, and you will need a van and an answering machine. Public liability insurance is important too. Unless you take a part payment in advance on larger jobs, you could run into credit-control problems. Many jobs will come through word of mouth, and it is worth cultivating friends in related fields – builders, electricians and so on – who can then refer business to you.

Pottery

Pottery evening courses are always very popular, and there are also more advanced residential courses in various parts of the country, but the Diploma in Ceramics offered by some technical colleges is by no means essential. If you want to earn a living in this form of craftwork, there will be a lot of initial outlay: you need a kiln as well as a potter's wheel (electrically powered is best in both cases, and they are not cheap), and some other items and materials. Study the *Ceramic Review* for secondhand equipment on sale.

Pottery can be a fire hazard; make sure you check the insurance cover for whatever premises you are using. It is worth checking on any local authority stipulations in your area, especially if you are using any power other than electricity; however, you can certainly convert a garage or large shed into a studio, as long as you have access to power and water.

As with any hand-produced items, you must have that elusive combination of individuality and style if you are to succeed in marketing yourself to the more expensive gift shops or selling your own products on market or antique stalls. Contact your local arts guild or association to see if there is a chance of your work being included in an exhibition. When you are established, you may even be able to market limited editions of your work through department stores.

Preserves

This tends to be a bit of a joke, associated by many with Women's Institutes, but there is business potential for homemade pickles, chutneys, marmalade, and mincemeat; the more individual (and preferably ancient) the recipes are, the better. Presentation is very important – go for unusual jars which will stand out in a line of similar products. If you are good enough, you can sell in bulk to the local delicatessens, or even to bigger shops, and achieve regular orders and a regular income.

Outlay is not high, but there are the usual legal restrictions associated with catering, and your jars *must* have properly printed labels detailing your name and address, a description of the contents, the exact weight, and the date of production.

Do not even think of competing with the big manufacturers of millions of jars; concentrate on marketing a quality product, and your outlets will be able to ask as much as twice the price.

Printing

One of the chief advantages of this sort of work is that it is very satisfying, which may help to compensate for the difficulties of making a living in what is a very competitive market. You cannot hope to compete with the High Street franchises in terms of equipment, or premises, so what kind of service can you offer from your garage or garden shed?

You will need to offer a variety of services – photocopying (rent a good machine, but never lease if you can avoid it; technological developments could make the machine you have obsolete and worthless), typing services, duplicating, concentrating on schools, voluntary groups and freelance individuals rather than businesses. The more contacts you already have among such groups, the better. Only when you are well established, and perhaps never, should you even consider investing capital in more expensive offset litho equipment and offering a full design and print service to business.

There are courses available on the craft side of printing (contact the London College of Printing in particular), and hand-printing machines are not too expensive. You might even think in terms of publishing illustrated limited editions of famous works, checking first that the copyright has expired, of course! This is a much riskier undertaking, but it might get you noticed at least.

Private investigation

Anybody can set themselves up as a private detective, though organizations such as the Association of British Investigators try to regulate standards by ensuring that at least potential applicants to the profession do not have criminal records, and have an adequate knowledge of the law. Contrary to popular opinion, it is by no means essential to have a background of work in the police force; if you have worked for a solicitor, or an insurance company, you may well have relevant knowledge. You will probably want to rent an office, but this can be discreetly above a shop and outlay need not be great apart from this.

Divorce is no longer such an important part of the investigator's work; more common would be the checking of alibis or insurance claims, or often the serving of writs. For the more sophisticated and established, a knowledge of electronic hardware and its applications in industrial counter-espionage or even the vetting of employees, could be a lucrative and expanding field. There is a great deal of variety, but not glamour, in such work.

Advertising is less likely to be a useful source of business than personal contact, hopefully garnered from past work experience. Make contact with local solicitors, establish their confidence in you, and you may be able to build up a string of regular connections. Charging rates are generally by the hour, and can be as high as £25 for the experienced professional.

Property letting agency

Residential lettings is a good business to move into if you have a relatively small amount of capital, because contracts can be signed and commission earned quite quickly; none the less, a background in estate agency is useful. You really need a High Street shop location and a smart office image, and much of your start-up capital will have to be spent on getting this right.

The most lucrative client is one whose work takes him or her abroad regularly and wants a tenant to look after the house as much as to make a profit; as with any agency work, the key is to match the tenant to the client – if all goes well, that client will come to the same agency again and again, and of course recommend you to friends, many of whom may be in similar situations. In this case, rent is collected and commission charged before it is passed on to the client;

one good means of finding a steady stream of potential clients is to keep in touch with the larger companies in your area, who may prefer to house executives temporarily in rented accommodation rather than fork out for huge hotel bills.

A more downmarket alternative, the accommodation agency, specializes in finding rented accommodation, usually for single people and often in the popular shared arrangement. Here the new tenant (or more usually, licensee; make sure you understand fully the various Rent Acts and devise suitable agreements accordingly) is charged a fee of perhaps two weeks' rent when a suitable place is found and the agreement is signed. This kind of agency may be more appropriate for you if you are based in a less affluent urban area, where there may be a large floating population of students and young single people.

Publicity services

You will have a background in marketing or publicity work, and good contacts among business people locally, or in your fields of interest. To begin with, you should aim to work in your clients' offices, perhaps for a set number of hours per week. This will save on telephone, secretarial and photocopying bills, since you will have access to your clients' facilities.

Concentrate on smaller firms who cannot afford to fund a full-time marketing or publicity post, but will pay you for perhaps one day per week to handle their public relations for them. You need to put together a good brochure – perhaps with a portfolio of your work – and mailshot, following up with telephone calls. Once you are established, contacts are everything in building up your business, and your aim could be to equip your own office with a range of facilities – fax, computer, secretarial staff – so that you can handle clients' publicity campaigns on a consultancy basis.

Expenses are limited at the outset, except that you will need to spend money on quality business stationery and your own publicity material – here, more than in any other business, your ability to sell yourself is what is going to count. Have good-quality business cards printed, but do not describe yourself as a consultant on these: potential clients will be put off by what sounds like a lot of money for not much work. Consultancy fees are based on your experience and skills, and can be as high as you can get away with, since a company can gain enormous benefits from just a few hours' work by somebody who really knows what they are about. When you are starting out, and working on clients' premises, you will have to think more in terms of the market salary rate for an executive of your calibre, and charge in proportion to that.

Rabbit farming

You should not attempt this as a full-time commercial venture until you have tried it out as a pilot project with a few doe rabbits. The first step will be to write to the Commercial Rabbit Association to obtain details of the courses and the practical guidance it can offer. Initial capital investment is high – apart from the cost of the rabbits themselves, their housing is likely to be out of your range unless you already have considerable outbuildings which you can adapt.

The Association should be able to help you with the essential task of finding guaranteed outlets for the rabbits; rabbits really are so prolific that, once the initial capital has been invested, you can produce huge numbers. But good management is crucial to the success of such a venture, and clearly you need to know that you have the affinity with the animals that will be a key ingredient.

The primary reason for breeding rabbits is as a source of meat, but changes in eating habits may make this a declining market. Make sure you are complying with legal requirements – you will have to register with your local authority, for example.

Roofing

You will probably have worked for a roofing contractor, and have a good knowledge of the kinds of roofs most prevalent in your locality. You can work either on a sub-contracted basis for building firms, or for private clients directly. Personal recommendation is important, because this is one of the businesses where there are problems with cowboys, so build up your contacts with other skilled tradespeople who might pass work on.

Initial capital requirements are not large: you want a van, ladders and some tools; you might also want to advertise in the local press and/or do a leaflet drop. Make sure private customers give you a deposit to cover the cost of materials. Obviously this is the kind of business which may thrive more easily in an area of older properties, and it should go without saying that you need a head for heights.

Shoe cleaning

This may not sound very glamorous, but the profit potential is greater than might at first appear. The key is to offer your services in large open-plan offices within large companies where a lot of people work in close proximity, and where you can clean a large number of pairs of shoes in quick succession, taking only a few minutes for each pair; City financial institutions are perhaps the best kind of arena. Speed is of course of the essence, and with a smart image and a bag for your equipment, a healthy hourly rate can be achieved.

As soon as you have established a strong demand for such a service, you should be looking both to increase staff (and to act, in effect, as an administrator, cleaning shoes yourself only when short of employees to do it for you), and also to expand the range of services offered. Such a business could even be combined with catering (the snack lunch service); be as flexible as you can, and take advantage of the fact that personal contact with a large number of clients gives you an opportunity to sell almost anything, and to offer almost any service, once you have gained the crucial trust.

Shoemaking

There is still a demand for independently designed and manufactured shoes in Britain, and there are courses available to start you off; contact the Clothing and Footwear Institute in the first instance. You do not need very much in the way of space or equipment, though you will need a heavy-duty sewing machine, for example.

As with any creative product, you have to take the plunge and carry your samples around the small upmarket shops, where the shoes you make might sell for £100 or more; once you build up a reputation with one or two of these, you may get regular commissions, and you should also build up contacts by visiting trade and fashion shows.

Because of the expense of the finished product, there is greater financial potential in shoes than in most craft businesses, but you have to believe in yourself and your talent.

Snack lunch service

Your customers will be the staff of small or medium-sized businesses, since larger firms will have their own staff restaurant; you will supply a menu of ready-made sandwiches, along with extras such as biscuits, soft drinks and crisps. Deliver to each firm at the same time each day, collecting orders for the following day; you will therefore be delivering against specific orders, but you should also carry an extra stock of your most popular sandwiches for casual sales. People should appreciate the convenience, and of course the quality, of the sandwiches, and should be prepared to pay more than they would in the High Street. Be as cheerful, and as flexible, as you can; there is no reason why you should not prepare practically any filling a person asks for.

You may find *The Grocer* useful for information on where to obtain ingredients wholesale. In any catering business, hours can be unsocial: you may have to rise very early to spend your mornings preparing the sandwiches. You must ensure that you comply with Environmental Health regulations, so contact your local authority before you begin trading – you will need transport which is used exclusively for food, for example.

Teas and refreshments

This is not a business for the fainthearted; it is very hard work, and requires considerable capital investment. You will need tables and chairs, trays, far more crockery than you think (because of breakages), as well as a freezer and kitchen supplies. And you will need to rent premises for a trial period of perhaps six months: clean, smart premises which can easily be spotted by passing motorists. You must get a copy of the Food Hygiene regulations from HMSO, and contact your local authority, who will need to inspect your premises.

The big advantage is that the market is almost guaranteed, as long as you take care not to site yourself too close to any similar kind of venture. There is no need for you to sell teas in a beautiful timber-framed cottage in a beautiful and unspoilt corner of England; indeed, the demand might be still greater in the heart of one of our large cities. There are always motorists, all year round, who are prepared to pay for an old-fashioned tea with china cups and scones with cream or jam.

You will have to work unsocial hours, for much of your business will arrive on Saturday and Sunday afternoons, though you should be able to find casual weekend staff without too much of a struggle.

Textile design

A design qualification from an art college is a great advantage; retail experience could also be helpful, especially if you have contacts with potential buyers as a result. Some courses are more commercially orientated than others and may offer opportunities to work with professionals on a short-term basis. Start-up costs are not high, though the use of screen-printing techniques to make up designs on to material is not cheap.

The hardest part is selling, and personal contact is always best: make up portfolios of your work, and strive to get appointments with key people in the retailing groups. Even the big chain stores who employ their own designers full-time still buy designs from outside, though unfortunately you only receive a flat payment for each design and not a royalty on the number of sales of the finished garment or product. Until you are well known to buyers, this is going to be very tough, but when you are well established you may be given regular commission work; it will not feel so creative, but it brings in money. Trade fairs are important; you may find it effective to use an agent to take your portfolio to all the shows, in exchange for a fat commission, but you should certainly aim for a personal presence as often as possible. Agents may be more useful for overseas trips, especially to New York. Study fashion and interior design magazines to keep abreast of trends, as well as the *DR: The Fashion Business*.

Tourist guiding

You must first study for one of the Blue Badges awarded by regional tourist boards after training courses of several months. If you already have a good knowledge of at least one foreign language (preferably a less common one, such as Japanese) that will be a tremendous initial advantage. Even after you have qualified you may find it useful to work for one of the large tour operators for a bit before branching out on your own, and to keep extending your areas of interest.

To create your own business, you will need to put together a smart letterhead, and try a direct mailshot to travel agents, tourist boards, local tourist information centres and tour operators. Be creative; put together suggested tours which are that bit different from the ones already on offer. Once you have got a reputation for bringing the local history alive to your clients, you may be able to pick up a lot of business through personal recommendation.

Contact the regional tourist boards in the first instance; this is one field in which entry is possible from a very wide variety of backgrounds. You should bear in mind that work will be heavily concentrated in the summer months, though less so in London where the competition for business is bound to be that much greater.

Toy making

There is a strong market for hand-made toys on traditional lines, such as rocking-horses; that said, a talent for woodwork or another craft skill may be the only qualification you need, though there are sometimes more specialized local courses in toy making available. Contact the British Toy Makers' Guild; it always looks good to be a member of such a body. It might help if you have experience of working in a toy shop, especially if you have contacts with potential buyers as a result.

Safety standards are important here: make sure you have a copy of the Toys (Safety) Regulations (there is a leaflet available from HMSO) and that you study these before you start using lead paint or similar prohibited materials.

You can sell your own work at craft fairs, in which case it is probably best to keep to simple designs. Or you can approach toy shops in your area, or the big London stores; the kudos you obtain from a contract with one of these could be of great benefit, but if you do enter into any such agreement it is of course essential that you have the capacity to deliver the requisite number of goods within the time specified. If you are aiming to sell directly to the public, editorial space in local newspapers or a mention on local radio will be much more valuable than straight advertising.

Translation services

You must have a thorough reading knowledge of at least one, and probably two, foreign languages; some business or technical knowledge could be useful, especially if you intend to specialize in particular industries. If you have friends or contacts who know other languages, and are prepared to do work for you on an occasional basis, you can improve the coverage of your service, and take a profit on their work. You will certainly need a good typewriter or word processor.

Again, this is ideal for a direct mailshot – try in particular the local business which imports or exports goods but is too small to need a permanent translation staff. Your local Chamber of Commerce may help you to find appropriate companies; send out a brochure, and follow up with a telephone call. Also try the British Overseas Trade Board; it may be prepared to recommend your services. Any client you meet or talk to should be kept on file; they may not have work for you just now, but when they do, they will remember you before they start looking around for somebody else. And remember the public sector – local courts, for example, may have work from time to time. As with any service based on the written word, it is no longer a disadvantage to be at a distance from London; modern communications have made it practicable for London firms to employ you, especially if you are cheaper. Join a business centre, so that you can put the fax number on your letterhead; it tells clients that you can present work quickly, wherever your base may be.

Good quality stationery and sales literature is vital. When you are starting out, you may find it difficult to charge your time per hour, but thinking in terms of what your client would pay a skilled translator full-time will help to focus you on the sort of figure you can aim at without embarrassment. And as with all such services, you are established when you are in demand and able, to some degree at least, to dictate your own charges.

You might be fed up with talk of 1992 everywhere, but translation is very obviously one area which is going to benefit.

Tree surgery

Tree surgery is a relatively new freelance occupation; you can work for private or public sector clients whose trees are diseased or simply too large. Contact the Forestry Training Council for relevant training courses, which are essential if you are to have an adequate knowledge of different types of trees and their problems; the Rural Development Commission should also be able to give advice on marketing and finance.

Start-up costs are not huge: you need a vehicle, ladders, chain saws, and equipment to allow you to climb trees safely. It is essential that you have insurance to cover you against damage you may cause to property or people. Charges will be based on an hourly rate, which will not be vast, but if you love trees, and thrive in dangerous situations, this could have great appeal.

Tutoring

If you have a degree or a teaching qualification, for example, or real and demonstrable knowledge and experience in a particular field (such as dancing or writing) you can advertise your services to potential pupils. You need no more than a quiet and comfortable room, and a supply of relevant reference material, but you may have to be prepared to advertise quite extensively at first, either in specialist journals or local newspapers, depending on the subject matter concerned. English for overseas businessmen is always in demand, and you should be able to command higher rates for such pupils, particularly if you are prepared to visit them rather than vice versa.

Teaching for school examinations is probably best avoided unless you are yourself an ex-schoolteacher with up-to-date information on the syllabus. However, when you are more established, you may like to consider correspondence courses, which can be very lucrative if you can find a gap in the market. Write to the Council for the Accreditation of Correspondence Colleges to see what is already on offer.

Upholstery

There is a demand for this, particularly in relation to the restoration of antiques, but you need some proper training, in curtains and loose covers as well as in upholstery proper: the basics can be learnt through the City and Guilds certificate or local college courses, but some practical work experience is also important before you branch out on your own.

You will need proper workshop premises, and transport, as well as a good deal of basic equipment: sewing-machines, shears, upholsterer's hammer, and so on. And you will need to be able to work quickly to turn round work and make a good profit. Try advertising in the Yellow Pages, and in your local newspapers, concentrating on the more affluent neighbourhoods. There is an Association of Master Upholsterers, and you may wish to join the Guild of Master Craftsmen as well.

Video production

There is an expanding market among smaller businesses for promotional and training videos. There are courses available on video production techniques, but any work experience in the field is likely to give you a better idea of what is involved on the ground. The key ingredients to success are the ability to interpret a client's needs in creative form, and the ability to sell yourself to the client.

You will not need to invest a great deal in video equipment at the outset, but it must be of good quality, and you will need smart business cards and promotional literature. Any mailshots and follow-ups you do will only succeed if you have examples of your work to show the client, so it is a great help if you can build up a small initial portfolio of videos made for your business friends. There may also be possibilities in the public or voluntary sector; the money will not be so good, but such commissions nevertheless give you valuable experience.

Window-cleaning

There is not a great deal to be said about window-cleaning that has not already been said in the section on market research and drawing up the business plan. As ever, it represents a sound, basic business, with the potential to develop into a larger organization employing a team of others, if you are prepared to work very hard. Believe it or not, the greatest problem is the temptation to take on far too much work, leading to exhaustion and disillusionment. It is much better to pace yourself; after all, if you are that much in demand, why not consider increasing your charges slightly?

USEFUL ADDRESSES

The following list of organizations and publications is by no means exhaustive; it simply represents those sources of information referred to elsewhere in this book. Such sources are a first port of call, and in most cases they will be able to suggest other lines of inquiry. But do remember to enclose a SAE when you write.

Please note that from May 1990 the STD codes for all telephone numbers in the London area will change to either (071) or (081), depending on whether the exchange concerned is in central or outer London. British Telecom will be happy to supply further details.

Antiques Trade Gazette, 17 Whitcomb Street, London WC2H 7PL (Tel. 01–930 7192)

Association of British Introduction Agencies, 29 Manchester Street, London W1 (Tel. 01–938 1011)

Association of British Investigators, 10 Bonner Hill Road, Kingston, Surrey (Tel. 01–546 3368)

Association of Independent Computer Specialists, 5 Bridge Avenue, Maidenhead, SL6 1RR (Tel. 0628–35913)

Association of Master Upholsterers, 564 North Circular Road, London NW2 (Tel. 01–452 4469)

British Antique Furniture Restorers' Association, 37 Upper Addison Gardens, London W14 8AJ (Tel. 01–603 5643)

British Decorators' Association, 45 Sheen Lane, London SW14 (Tel. 01–876 4415)

British Franchise Association, Franchise Chambers, 75a Bell Street, Henley on Thames, Oxfordshire, RG9 2BD (Tel. 0491–578049)

British Handknitting Association, PO Box CR4, Leeds LS7 4NA

British Institute of Professional Photography, 2 Amwell End, Ware, Hertfordshire, SG12 9HN (Tel. 0920–4011)

British List Brokers' Association, Springfield House, Princess Street, Bedminster, Bristol, BS3 4EF (Tel. 0272–666900)

British Overseas Trade Board, 1 Victoria Street, London SW1 (Tel. 01–215 7877)

British Toy Makers' Guild, 240 The Broadway, London SW19 (Tel. 01–878 9055)

Campaign, 22 Lancaster Gate, London W2 3LY (Tel. 01–402 4200)

Ceramic Review, 21 Carnaby Street, London W1 (Tel. 01–439 3377)

Clothing & Footwear Institute, 71 Brushfield Street, London E1 (Tel. 01–247 1696)

Commercial Rabbit Association, Whitemantle, 172 Reading Road South, Church Crookham, Aldershot, Hampshire, GU13 0AE

Co-Operative Development Agency, Broadmead House, 21 Panton Street, London SW1Y 4DR (Tel. 01–839 2985)

Council for the Accreditation of Correspondence Colleges, 27 Marylebone Road, London NW1 5JS (Tel. 01–935 5391)

Council for Licensed Conveyancers, Golden Cross House, Duncannon Street, London WC2N 4JF (Tel. 01–210 4604)

Design Council, 28 Haymarket, London SW1 (Tel. 01–839 8000)

DR: The Fashion Business, 100 Avenue Road, London NW3 3TP (Tel. 01–935 6611)

Driving Instructors' Association, Lion Green Road, Coulsdon, Surrey (Tel. 01–660 3333)

Federation of Master Builders, 33 John Street, London WC1 (Tel. 01–242 7583)

Forestry Training Council, Forestry Commission, 231 Corstorphine Road, Edinburgh, EH12 7AT (Tel. 031–334 8083)

Forum of Private Business Ltd, Francis House, Francis Street, London SW1 (Tel. 01–828 5950)

Gaming Board for Great Britain, Berkshire House, High Holborn, London WC1 (Tel. 01–240 0821)

Graphology Centre, 9b Hyde Park Mansions, Cabbell Street, London NW1 (Tel. 01–262 0198)

The Grocer, 5/7 Southwark Street, London SE1 1RQ (Tel. 01–407 6981)

Guild of Master Craftsmen, 166 High Street, East Sussex, BN7 1YE (Tel. 0273–478449)

HMSO, St Crispins, Duke Street, Norwich NR3 1PD (Tel. 0603–622211)

Industrial Common Ownership Movement, Vassali House, 20 Central Road, Leeds 1, West Yorkshire (Tel. 0532–461737)

Institute of Chartered Accountants in England and Wales, Chartered Accountants Hall, Moorgate Place, London EC2P 2BJ (Tel. 01–628 7060)

Institute of Heraldic & Genealogical Studies, 82 Northgate, Canterbury, Kent (Tel. 0227–68664)

Institute of Horticulture, 80 Vincent Square, London SW1 (Tel. 01–834 4333)

Institute of Plumbing, 64 Station Lane, Hornchurch, Essex (Tel. 04024–72791)

The Lady, 40 Bedford Street, London WC2E 9ER (Tel. 01–379 4717)

Landscape Institute, Nash House, 12 Carlton House Terrace, London SW1Y 5AH (Tel. 01–839 4044)

London College of Fashion, 20 John Princes Street, London W1 (Tel. 01–629 9401)

London College of Furniture, 41 Commercial Road, London E1 (Tel. 01–247 1953)

London College of Printing, Elephant & Castle, London SE1 (Tel. 01–735 8484)

London Enterprise Agency, 4 Snow Hill, London EC1A 2DL (Tel. 01–236 3000)

London & Provincial Antique Dealers' Association, 3 Cheval Place, London SW7 (Tel. 01–584 7911)

Mushroom Growers' Association, Agriculture House, Knightsbridge, London SW1 (Tel. 01–235 5077)

The Musician, 239 Shaftesbury Avenue, London WC2H 8EH (Tel. 01–240 5749)

National Extension College, 18 Brooklands Avenue, Cambridge, CB2 2HN (Tel. 0223–316644)

National Farmers' Union, Agriculture House, Knightsbridge, London SW1 (Tel. 01–235 5077)

National Federation of Health & Beauty Therapists, PO Box 36, Arundel, West Sussex, BN18 0SW

National Inspection Council for Electrical Installation Contracting, Vintage House, 36 Albert Embankment, London SE1 (Tel. 01–735 1322)

Practical Woodworking, Hatfield House, Stamford Street, London SE1 9LS (Tel. 01–261 6731)

Retail Jeweller, 100 Avenue Road, London NW3 (Tel. 01–935 6611)

Rural Development Commission, 141 Castle Street, Salisbury, Wiltshire, SP1 3TP (Tel. 0722–336255)

Shoe & Leather News, 84 Great Eastern Street, London EC2 (Tel. 01–739 2071)

Society of Genealogists, 14 Charterhouse Buildings, London EC1 (Tel. 01–251 8799)

Society of Licensed Conveyancers, 32 Craignish Avenue, London SW16 4RN (Tel. 01–679 1619)

Soil Association, 86 Colston Street, Bristol 1, Avon (Tel. 0272–290661)

Wool Secretariat (International), 6 Carlton Gardens, London SW1 (Tel. 01–930 7300)

Sample business plan

Note: the projected profit and loss account and cash-flow forecast which relate to this plan will be found on pages 48 and 52. The purpose of this sample business plan is to illustrate one possible way of setting out the relevant information; detailed market information, and information on accounting procedures and recent sales results, which would certainly be required in a live situation, have not been included here. Similarly, the fact that the partners of this firm have budgeted for the purchase of computer/word processors illustrates that there are certain kinds of businesses where this would be justified; it should certainly *not* be taken as an indication that this would necessarily be appropriate for other types of business.

Background

Heritage Research Services is currently operating on a sole trader basis from premises at Zippy Business Centre, Deadend Street, London SE29. The major business activity is ancestry research on behalf of individual clients all over the world, but research is also carried out into the histories of houses and businesses. The business began trading in January 1990, but an injection of new capital and staff will become, in effect, a start-up situation. It is proposed that a limited company be established to formalise this new start.

The short-term objectives of the business are to increase available capital to allow for growth into new markets, and to increase staff to service a large number of clients more efficiently. Longer-term growth should then be self-financing, but it is not proposed to diversify significantly from the company's core activities.

A small suite of offices in the business centre has been budgeted for in the projections, and is likely to be sufficient for all foreseeable future needs; the budget figure is inclusive of rates, power, telephone and insurances.

Personnel

The business was set up by Mr A, who is now to be joined by Ms B. Both are history graduates with several years first-hand experience in historical and genealogical research. Each is to invest £2500 in the business, giving them an equal share in the equity. They have also decided on a broad division of responsibilities: Mr A will be responsible for the commissioning of research from freelance agents throughout the world, quality control, progress chasing and client relations; Ms B's central preoccupations will be report writing, marketing, and the supervising of accounting and office administration functions. The two partners/directors have agreed to take no more than the equivalent of £10,000 per annum out of the business in the early stages, and this has been budgeted for in the profit and loss account.

In the initial stages it is proposed to employ only a part-time bookkeeper/administrator, since the purchase of two inexpensive word processors will enable the partners/directors to type most of their own reports and correspondence. The partners recognize that this purchase of capital equipment at the outset can only be justified in terms of savings elsewhere, but submit that the volume of writing involved is such that it will be a huge advantage for the firm if the management is self-sufficient in this regard.

Research work will be carried out by freelance researchers in different locations around the country, and this figure increases directly in proportion to the volume of business, since one third of any client's budget is generally devoted to research.

Market

Ancestry research has boomed as a leisure subject in the last fifteen years, and as the number of active participants has grown, so too has the number of those who would like to know more about their ancestry, cannot afford the time to pursue the matter and are prepared to pay for professional research.

Most professionals operate on a freelance basis in one or more locations; only a very few companies are able to offer a complete national and international service, co-ordinating the work of these freelance researchers, interpreting the results of research and producing an attractive final report for the client. The partners have worked for two other companies in the field, neither of which was capable of turning work around quickly enough or cheaply enough to generate a really high level of customer satisfaction; a high proportion of income in this line of work can be expected from renewals and referrals, if customer satisfaction is achieved. For this reason, the business intends to devote more energy than any of its competitors towards keeping and building on existing clients.

The two other companies have an annual turnover in excess of £150,000. Since the partners have inside information on the advertising response of those firms, a major initial effort will be to attract business away from them by advertising more effectively in some of the same places, principally glossy 'heritage' and tourist publications circulating throughout the English-speaking world. It will be seen that substantial resources have been earmarked for this advertising campaign, especially in the early months of expansion. The firm does already have a few North American clients, but it is not proposed to concentrate on developing this export market until the firm is much better established in Britain.

The initial turnover target in this first year will be the break-even point of £75,000, which is felt to be realistic; it represents less than 25 per cent of the market share, even on the assumption that the market does not continue to grow on the pattern of recent years. The service offered has already been market-tested, in the sense that Heritage Services already generates enough income to pay for the salary of one partner; moreover, clients are more than satisfied with the quality and speed of the service, and there is already evidence that higher advertising response rates have been achieved than the major competitors.

Finance

The projections will illustrate the need for an investment of £10,000 capital to enable the following specific needs to be met:

(a) Salary payments to the second partner/director
(b) Purchase of two computer/word processors, for reasons discussed earlier
(c) An extensive initial advertising campaign to seize the initiative from major competitors

Since £5000 of the capital requirement will be met by the partners, it is suggested that the remaining £5000 be made available as a formal term loan. We have previously pointed out that Heritage Services is already trading and supporting one member of staff; although no income has been projected for the first two months, this is a pessimistic view and it is likely that the full £5000 will never in fact be required. However, to allow flexibility we suggest that no capital repayments be made in the first year, and that thereafter the capital be repaid at the rate of £500 per quarter.

Index of business ideas

Index of business ideas

General index